Don't Follow Me, I'm The Leader!

dave dupre

Dedication

To those of you who were told countless times that you would never see your dreams come true.

To those of you who thought the decisions you've made in the past or ones made by others meant that you would never rise again to fulfill your destiny.

To those of you who's vision has been buried under the strain of life's disappointments.

To those of you who have stepped back to let others lead because you've been taught to lose.

IT'S NOT OVER!

"Sometimes the mistaken brush stroke we make on life's canvas, God uses to create His greatest masterpiece."

- dave dungan -

Table Of Contents

Acknowledgements...*ix*

Foreword..*xi*

Introduction...*xiii*

SECTION ONE—

    • The Pretender...3
    • I Want to Come in Second 5
    • *X* Marks the Spot 7
    • Do You See What I'm Saying? 9

    Life Application Review.....................................11

SECTION TWO—

    • If I Ain't Got It, You Don't Need It 15
    • It's Only $19.99..17
    • A Ticket to the Parade 19
    • Jacko the Baboon 21

    Life Application Review.....................................23

SECTION THREE—

    • Have I Told You Lately That I Love You? 27
    • Know When to Exit the Wave 29
    • I Thought You Turned the Gas Off 31
    • Let the Rough Edges Drag 33

    Life Application Review.....................................35

SECTION FOUR—

- Who in the #@!!* Are You? 39
- Try Before You Pry 41
- The Word for the Day Is Retention. 43
- Recalculating 45

Life Application Review. 47

SECTION FIVE—

- A Bird in the Hand. 51
- Absitively-Posilutely 53
- Are You Hurt or Injured? 55
- The Twelve-Foot Shuffle 57

Life Application Review. 59

SECTION SIX—

- Hey, Coach! 63
- Who's the Boss? 65
- Talented, but Not a Play Maker 67
- Exactly the Same, Just Different 69

Life Application Review. 73

SECTION SEVEN—

- Yeah, I Hear You, But . . .. .77
- Slow Is Smooth. 79
- Lowering Your Standards to Up Your Average 81
- Slow Motion Is Better Than No Motion 83

Life Application Review. 85

SECTION EIGHT—

- The Voice of Reason 89
- The Art of Teaching Experience 91
- Surviving Is Not Growing 95
- Preparing the Square Peg for the Round Hole 97

Life Application Review 99

SECTION NINE—

- The Stabilizing Factor 103
- How's My Driving? 105
- The Best Excuse, Ever! 107
- Hocus Focus 109

Life Application Review 111

SECTION TEN—FIVE KEY PITFALLS OF LEADERS

- Approval 115
- Neglect 117
- Abuse 119
- Influence 121
- Alienation 123

A Final Thought 125

About the Author 127

Acknowledgements

To Pete and Carol: Thank you for your amazing examples of leadership. The two of you have given to so many the tools to create for themselves new beginnings in the arena of leadership. You are awesome examples for all of us to follow. Thanks for being who you are.

To Diane: You have been with us from the beginning. Your accomplishments as a business leader and devoted friend have changed the lives of so many. You are truly an inspiration to all who seek to reach for the impossible dream.

To Donnie and Denise: As business leaders, you have set the bar high. As friends, you have set it even higher. You have built your business and more importantly your lives on character. This has set you apart and has made you a gift to those who have the privilege of calling you friends. And Donnie, I still think you should run for Mayor.

To Charlie and Mary Frances: You exemplify the true meaning of sacrifice. Your unselfish passion for giving has opened so many doors for those with dreams. As leaders, you have equipped others to set higher standards. We are forever grateful for the gift of your friendship.

To Ray and Ginette: Thank you for being a champion to all who have dared to dream of greater things. You have invested so much into so many with expectations only of seeing others soar. Your influence has truly enriched all of us who desire to grasp hold of our destinies.

I have always loved that picture that shows the turtle perched on top of a fence post. I'm amazed at leaders who say they've made it on their own with no help from others. It isn't true and never will be. Even those who were told they would never make it or amount to anything in life were inspired by those very influences. The drive to prove the naysayer wrong created the passion that brought those men and women to the top of their games. No, everyone is who he/she is because of another's influence good or bad and no matter how painful.

There have been positive and negative influences in my life as well. Those influences also helped to shape who I am. The greatest of these influences is my family. Their sacrifices and encouragement have kept my course true. Debbie, thank you for your tenacity and strength, you are such a gift to me and the boys. Your character has always inspired me to forge ahead even when others brought to me great disappointment. Thank you for always believing in me. I love you!

Foreword

During the past 25 years I have read several hundred books on leadership and motivation. Dave Dungan's first book, "An Offering Made by Fire", reached my heart like no other. It helped clear the fog from my vision so that I could refocus on my mission of helping others develop their full potential.

Have you ever questioned your potential to achieve? Have you ever been disappointed by "leaders" you were following? Have you ever been let down by people you poured part of your life into in hopes of having them succeed? If you, as a leader, are looking to have your passion restored, Dave's new book will help lift the fog, help you focus, and reset your inner GPS so you can not only continue on your journey of success but assist others as well.

In his new book, Dave shares the basic foundation of sustained success based on timeless principles that he has utilized over the past three decades. Dave has the gift of simplifying these complex principles so they may be applied on every level of leadership to develop winning teams. Whether your arena is business, ministry, education, politics or sports, you will learn that the key is not only having the right people on your team, but also focusing on the strengths of those individuals for the benefit of the organization as a whole.

My son, Pierre, often times will ask me, "Dad, what is your source for such information?" Who is Dave Dungan? Dave is a leader who has dedicated his life in developing and teaching people to expand their leadership skills that incorporates taking as many along with them as they can. Dave illustrates that success is a journey and not a destination, and offers guidance in spite of the obstacles and bumps we might encounter along the way. He explains various methods of building strong foundations so we can thrive in the midst of the winds of adversity.

You have heard that knowledge is the power needed to change lives, but Dave explains that it is the personal application of that knowledge that has the power to change lives and empower others to succeed. Don't let the PAST determine your FUTURE. Read and apply the success principles that Dave shares with us in this book. Leadership is not controlling others but empowering them to function as part of a growing organization.

"Don't Follow Me, I'm The Leader" gives us the internal fortitude to keep growing and to forge ahead on our journeys in spite of our obstacles and weaknesses. This book will equip us with the skills and the process to realize our DREAMS!

Enjoy your journey!

Ray Dumais, M.Ed.
Former Adult Education Director
Speaker and Entrepreneur
Hooksett, New Hampshire

Introduction

A very successful businessman once told me that there was something a lot more intoxicating than money could ever be. At the time, I thought what could be more intoxicating than lots of money? I later learned by watching him what he was actually talking about. It was influence! He told me that money gives you influence and influence gives you power. I saw firsthand what money could do, and I saw the power it yielded as well. That influence made things happen all around him. He was treated differently from everyone else because everyone knew that with a stroke of his pen he could change their futures. As a result, he knew and expected that kind of treatment no matter where he went. It really was most intoxicating, at least on the surface.

Many years have gone by since then, and I see things a little more clearly now. Looking back, I realize that this gentleman had greater powers than even he realized. That power was the ability to empower others. How much greater a man he would have been had he recognized in others their potential and then invested in their futures. I'm not talking just about money, but about instruction and mentoring, passing on knowledge and providing opportunities to let others spread their wings to see how high they could soar. There can be no greater fulfillment than to have scores of people around you that you have helped reach their full potential. Now that's intoxicating!

So you too are in a position of influence. You have the power to affect the lives of those around you. You have a decision to make. You have a choice! Will you seize every opportunity for everything to be about you, or will you seize every opportunity to empower those around you? If you choose the latter, then you will be a great leader and will instill in those within your sphere of influence the desire to impart the same. What could be more rewarding than to be the leader of leaders?

Every true leader must ask themselves some very important questions. The first is: Do I have the passion? This is the engine that will drive your success. You will soon find that passion equips you to answer the second question and that is: Can you cast vision? Others must be able to see where you're going if they are to follow. Motivation will only go so far, but if others can see it, then passion will also begin to drive them as well. You must also ask yourself the question: Have I forced leadership upon myself or have others placed me there? True leaders are seldom self-made. Circumstances and events call them to this position, and they hone their skills as they grow under the influence of mentors.

You will find as you read on that there is a big difference between those who are in charge and those who truly lead. Where are you leading those who follow? There is only one true answer to this question and that is: you are leading them to empower others. At the end of the day, it is not important whether or not you made it to the top. What's really important is how many are standing there with you! You must also ask yourself: What am I using as a standard of leadership? *Character* should be the answer to this question. It is the greatest of foundations upon which to build your future. This too should answer the question as to whether or not you are for sale, not to others or even the competition but to opportunities that might cause you to compromise and question who you really are. And finally, having answered these questions, turn around. Is anyone following you?

This is just the beginning. There is so much more to leadership than the usual applications that you've learned. What you seldom learn about will become your most treasured assets. I have placed in this book the simple applications for possessing some of those treasures. What you do now with this information can position you not only to reach your goals but empower you to take many others with you. And that, dear leader, is something you must experience to understand! So get out your notebook and let me take you on a couple of life's experiences that could save you a great deal of frustration and maybe even some regret. Lead on.

—A Leader—

"Good character is more to be praised than outstanding talent. Most talents are, to some extent, a gift. Good character, by contrast, is not given to us. We have to build it piece by piece—by thought, choice, courage and determination."
—John Luther

"Character is the foundation stone upon which one must build to win respect. Just as no worthy building can be erected on a weak foundation, so no lasting reputation worthy of respect can be built on weak character."
—R. C. Samsel

Without character a leader is nothing more than someone who has been placed in charge. A true leader is someone who has the power of influence who can in turn empower others to reach their full potential and then find fulfillment in doing it. Character must be what true leadership is built on. Though there are many great books on success and leadership, hopefully this one will help you see yourself through the eyes of those who follow you.

I'm sure that most of you are familiar with the Burj Al Arab Hotel in Dubai. Built by South African contractors and currently the tallest hotel in the world, it is considered to be one of the great wonders of the world made by man. The engineering and architectural design was a first. Considered an impossible feat by most, the Burj Al Arab now stands as the only self-proclaimed seven-star hotel in the world.

The important information that I desire for you to receive is in the creation of its foundation. The engineers pumped sand into an area 920 feet off shore to create the man-made island. Because there was no stone to secure the foundation, the builders drove into the sand concrete piles that were 130 feet long. The settling of the sand in turn gripped the piles, securing them as if they were in concrete. The foundation was secured from erosion by building concrete honeycombs around the island. This was to protect it from the pounding waves brought in by the raging tides. There were more than two million, five hundred thousand cubic feet of concrete and nine thousand tons of steel. It took more than three years to create the man-made island and its foundation and less than three years to erect the building. It would have literally been impossible for such a structure to exist without the strength of such a sure foundation.

This is true for the leader as well, and that sure foundation is character. It doesn't matter if you are attempting to recreate something that already exists or building something that people say can't be built. You will be able to prove them wrong if you are building your future on the foundation of great character. Just as the engineers of the Dubai Hotel secured a sub-foundation, they also secured a surface protection that would ensure that over the course of time the structure would not be moved. As leaders you too have made decisions as well as sacrifices that have contributed to the foundation of your character. Those decisions, no matter how difficult, and the sacrifices, no matter how painful, have established in you a foundation of great character. There are many great leaders who have had deep foundations but allowed the constant pounding of surface motion to erode them away until that foundation crumbled.

As a leader you may find it easy as well as profitable to hone your trade as a manipulator. I hope not! Leadership is a gift, a gift to be given to others in the form of empowerment. The choice will be yours. Heed the truth of others and build a legacy that will last for generations instead of taking a quick trip to the top. Your responsibility is to equip others so that they may reach their full potential and inspire others to follow as well. You may find it more satisfying than any goal you have ever tried to reach.

"Losing to a better opponent may make you a better competitor; but losing to you is unacceptable. Never, ever quit on you!"
                                                              - dave dungan

Section One

The Pretender

You have probably heard the cliché, **"Fake it till you make it,"** but in the world of true leadership, there is no room for phonies. I remember a TV show that aired every week called *The Pretender*. It was about a young man who from a boy was a part of this secret organization that was developing gifted minds to create scenarios of all kinds in order to control certain events. The pretender could go into any profession and in a matter of hours was better at it than those who have had the training for years. What was amazing about the whole thing was his level of confidence. Spend a few minutes with the guy, and you were convinced to let him do brain surgery on you. Sound familiar? Yeah, I have met a few of them myself.

As a leader you must learn early that if you have weaknesses, you don't have to advertise them, but you certainly don't have to pretend you don't have them either. There are plenty of talented people you can surround yourself with who are more than capable of making things happen. I also fear that there is a very dark and powerful ability these pretenders have as leaders and that is the power of *manipulation*. This has got to be one of the most divisive tools a leader can have. Pretenders have to use it because they do not have great character. He/she is a fake and full of so many secrets that if the secrets were to come out in public, nobody would follow them.

Don't sell yourself or those you influence out to manipulation. Don't let other leaders tell you it is a necessary tool of negotiation either. A great leader will not stoop to manipulation; they will cast vision and work a plan they really believe in. You are free to navigate through difficult waters, but manipulation stands on the shoulders of deception. Remember that. You don't have to know how to do everything; you just have to know how to get everything done, and that is usually accomplished by having the right people in the right places. Remember that as a company you will never have *corporate manifestation* until you have *individual revelation.* As each individual gets it, the corporation expresses it.

It is imperative, therefore, to know clearly what your plan is and who it will take to make it happen. True success in leadership will ultimately be defined as to whether or not you *empowered* those under you to reach their full potential. If you do, you will succeed at whatever you do. The two very important things to remember about *pretending* are: don't do it, and really, please don't do it! You are better than that.

I Want to Come in Second

Destiny is not a matter of chance; it is a matter of choice. It is not a thing to be waited for; it is a thing to be achieved.
—William Jennings Bryan

I remember reading that quote on a plaque in a novelty store. Webster's definition of *destiny* is simply "the predetermined course of events considered as something beyond human power or control." Now, you could argue the fact that it appears that some just fall into destiny while others spend a lifetime chasing it. In either case steps were taken and events transpired to put both in position for destiny to meet up with them. No one should ever settle for just anything, let alone second best. We have all been given gifts, talents, and abilities to use to add to the quality of life all around us. What makes the difference is how we use these gifts to their full potential. It has been said by many great leaders that preparation precedes promotion. I believe this to be a fact also. With that being said, would it not also explain why some were in a position to step into their destiny when it showed up? Absolutely! All that you are has been shaped by the influences that are around you. The words that have been spoken to you and the personal conflict of life that you've endured have all affected your gifting and talent. For some there's not been enough positive influence around them to keep them moving forward, and they fall captive to lies and defeat. For others there has been the constant affirmation that they will never be able to lead and must step back and let others lead. How difficult this must be because while others dream without limitation these people can only aspire to a certain point. No, never settle for second best when everything in you is calling you to a different level. Remember, who has ever trained to run a race without the expectation and drive of winning?

You are reading this book because you are a leader or have a passion to be one. According to Mr. Webster, a leader is defined as someone who has power and influence over others. I believe that a leader is someone who *empowers* others to discover and use their talents to their full potential. This encompasses a great deal of responsibility because what most of you don't realize as leaders is that you usually don't manage a product; you manage people's lives. You have to navigate around the events that are happening in the lives of others to get them to operate at their highest potential. This takes a great deal of focus and skill. I have learned from others that to be a great leader you have to pursue your passion and people have to be your passion. If you simply want to be the head of something, then you can join the countless pretenders who do the same. There are plenty of them out there.

What of success? I have come up with three truths about success. The first is that it is never a constant, second it is relative, and third it is circumstantial. As to its lack of consistency, success may be held one moment and taken away the next. Success is relative to a focus. You may be great at business but fail as a husband/wife, father/mother, or friend. And not everyone holds success to the same standard. In any set of circumstances, you may be a huge winner in another's eyes, or you may be a loser.

So how will you measure your success? This is not complicated! If you use your talents, gifts, and abilities to help coach others to reach their full potential, then you can never lose. If you respect the power of influence and pursue your passion, you will find more fulfillment than you imagined possible, and, most importantly, you will be a great leader.

"*X*" Marks the Spot

I have heard for so many years from certain great leaders the old adage, "You have to start from where you're at." It's true by the way. One of the most frustrating barriers to break through is starting from where you're at. It is, I believe, human nature to want to get to a particular place before you try to move toward your goals. People often say, "If I can just do so-and-so or do this before that, I'll be ready." The truth is you end up missing windows of opportunity that may never come again. Don't get me wrong, you do have to project and plan, but not at the expense of moving forward.

As I look back, I realize that time has become my worst enemy. As a young man, I viewed the future as if I had an eternity to fulfill my dreams. Now I have come to the realization that I have missed opportunities that will not come again. As far as regret, I cannot say because I cannot predict the future, but I can say that I have not done all that I had wished to accomplish, at least not yet. It is essential that you surround yourself with those who will push you. Without the constant voice of encouragement, you will remain safe in what you are doing. Safe is not necessarily the best place to be.

As a leader you have to step back and assess where you're at. You have to take inventory of your resources. Who are the people you network with, and how can they assist you in going to the next level? Granted, your starting point may not be the ideal place, but you can still move in the direction you want to go. The important thing is that when you focus on action, your energy is being spent on progress and not on where you need to be before you can begin.

The second assessment you need to make is of yourself. Where's your head right now? How many excuses have you come up with for why you're not where you're supposed to be? Listen, most of them are probably very good excuses, but remember that they're keeping you from your purpose. Sometimes the past—with all of its decisions whether right or wrong—can keep you from seeing the future. But what if…? Oh, forget what if and all of the woulda, coulda, and shoulda's because they're irrelevant at this moment. You are here now! Blaming someone else only makes you feel less guilty for the moment; it changes nothing. Remember, as long as you're looking back, you'll be stumbling through your future.

What about your attitude? I'm not talking about mind over matter, either. You know, if you don't mind, it doesn't matter! No, I'm talking about the true passion for where you are going; that drive that allows you to see through all of the setbacks. If you don't see where you're going, then you cannot obtain your destination. And the truth is no one else will see it for you. This is so important for you to see as a leader. You may be going up against some huge odds right now, but don't quit. Acknowledge to the world that this may be where you are, but it is not where you're going to be. It's just a place and nothing more. Remember that the word *nowhere* is made up of the two separate words: *now* and *here*. No matter how difficult the present is, it's simply a launching pad to the future. It's simply the starting point.

You know, I'm convinced that if you'd handed Picasso a box of crayons, he would still have created a masterpiece. It's just what was in him. A leader is the same way. If you put a leader into a situation, he or she will change the atmosphere as well as the outcome of that situation. Others will just sit and discuss all of the reasons why they did nothing. And most of them will be satisfied with the outcome. You are different; it is unacceptable for you to allow excuses to ruin your masterpiece. What's in your hands right now? What ever it is, use it. Start right now, right where you're at, to move toward your dream. If you cannot lead yourself, how will you lead others? Yeah, you are here, but it's not where you are going to stay; it's simply your starting point.

Do You See What I'm Saying?

There is nothing more frustrating than to give instructions to someone and have those instructions be interpreted incorrectly. It certainly must be due to incompetence, right? Right! And it's usually the fault of the leader. So take a deep breath and take this stuff in because it will save you a lot of frustration.

During my time in leadership conferences and the like, I learned so much about becoming a great leader, but there was one particular set of lessons I held onto as invaluable. There is nothing more important than successful communication. I'm not talking about the transfer of information. I'm talking about the comprehension of information. There is a very big difference! Let me explain by using a word you will come to love as a leader. It's the word **delineate.** You'll better understand its importance if you see it in action.

Suppose I'm your leader, and we have a project to accomplish. I tell you after much thought that the solution to our project is a car. So as the leader I delegate this task to you. You, of course, get with your team, and after a short period of time, you find a car and drive up in a 1975 Plymouth Volare. (Yeah, you really do need to look this car up to know what I'm talking about.) Now, when I walk out and see the car, I freak! I turn to you and say, "I asked for a car, and you bring me this piece of junk?" You in turn are confused because you thought you had done what I had asked you to do and you did it in a timely fashion! By now, I'm losing it because what I expected you to bring me was a dark blue 2011 Aston Martin with gray hand sown leather interior, not a rusty 1975 Plymouth Volare.

As the leader I'm frustrated because I don't understand why my go-to person didn't know exactly what I wanted. You get it already, don't you? It's just that simple. Proper delineation would have been for me to tell you that I wanted a dark blue 2011 Aston Martin with gray hand sown leather interior, you would have pulled up in one, and we could have all celebrated together. In this case, as the leader, the fact that I got a Volare rather than an Aston Martin was my fault.

There are too many influences that affect proper communications. Delineation prevents outside influences from mixing up the task at hand. Not everyone sees what you are saying just because you are saying it. One of the greatest attributes of a leader is the ability to get people to see inside their heads so that they anticipate movement in a unison flow. As the leader it is your responsibility to make sure things get done and done right. Remember that no one leaves the room until everyone has his or her job assignment and clear—and I mean crystal clear—instructions. It really is great to be a leader if everyone knows where you're going. After all, I would hope that you want to take them with you, right?

Life Application Review

Section One

Remember that you are who you are. If you need to be more (and most of the time you will), make the necessary adjustments to equip yourself to go to the next level. Usually, the only person who doesn't know you're faking it is you. You are (or you're going to be) a leader because you feel along with others that you have the abilities and necessary talents to influence the lives of those around you. Decide what is needed the most to bring others to your level. There is nothing wrong with not having all of the answers or the skills to do everything. Being a leader doesn't mean that you have all the answers and skills. It means you bring people up who can bring strength to your weakness and plug in skills to your less skillful areas. It is all about empowering those within your scope of influence.

If you are going to sit around and wait for destiny, then find a comfortable chair and relax, because you are going to be sitting for a very long time. If you know what you want to do, then go after it. Don't plan to come in second because that's not planning to win. Make destiny catch up with you because you're busy getting ready for it. Sharpen your skills, find that place of focus, and set your sights on your goals and then go after them. Reaching a place of leadership doesn't mean you have to destroy others to get there. Being a true leader means you are bringing people with you.

The best way to move ahead is to accept where you're at. Sometimes this is the most difficult thing to do. If ever there was a foundation to build from, it is this truth. Denial is the greatest supporter of procrastination. *If I could just get to this place, I could do better.* Well, where you're at is a place too. And if you can move from where you are, then you are on your way to where you want to go.

Communication is one of the greatest tools we have as a society. In fact we could not survive without it. Remember, there is a difference between information and the understanding of information. It's called comprehension. Make sure that communication is one of the most fluent tools you posses. If those who work with you can understand what you say, then you will most definitely accomplish a great deal. If not, then you will spend the majority of the time making excuses and finding someone to blame. Remember that you must become the master of delineation. Do you see what I'm saying?

Section Two

If I Ain't Got It, You Don't Need It

In a small hardware store called Herb's Hardware in Trussville, Alabama, hung a sign that stated, **"If I Ain't Got It, You Don't Need It!"** Herb liked to believe that he had everything you could possibly need to fix your problem. And for the most part he did. That sign reminded me often of my dad who is probably the smartest man I have ever known. I remember when I was young helping him with some of his projects and then going with him to the store to buy a particular tool for a job he was working on. When we asked the parts guy for the tool, he would at times tell us there was no such tool. My dad would smile and say, well there soon will be. We would return home, and he would start to work on making the tool we needed to finish the job. I watched him do it over and over again.

In watching my Dad work, I realized over time that the finished project never mattered as much as the journey he took to finish it. He spent more time showing people the tool that he made than he did talking about the finished project. I often thought to myself that he probably hoped that there wasn't a tool for the job just so he could make one! As a leader you will constantly come up with new vision and ideas that are cutting edge. You will have opportunities to pioneer new territory. It will be your responsibility to make it happen. There may be no patterns or molds to go by, and you will have people say, "Sorry, you can't do it because there is no such thing." You cannot allow that kind of thinking to cause you to put off your ideas or delay the cutting-edge projects. Make the tool to complete the project.

Persistence has to be your close companion because sometimes you may be the only one who believes in the project. I can remember countless times reading about successful people and how they arrived at success. When these men and women were questioned about how they made it, they without fail say: persistence. Never give up, no matter what! You be the one to make something that empowers others to reach their goals and full potential.

One of the most rewarding things you can experience as a leader is to empower someone else to obtain his or her dreams and to use your tools to do so! Your confidence in where you're going is the perfect atmosphere for creativity. It is in this place that you are able to take thought and hold it in your hands. So, if you can't find the tool, then make it. If they do have it, then make it a better one.

It's Only $19.99

How many times have you sat up late watching all those infomercials and found yourself guessing the price for the product before they announced it? It seems like everything offered is only $19.99. Let's face it man, it's really twenty bucks! Presentation is everything! For some reason $19.99 just sounds less expensive than $20. We're talking just a penny difference, but the way the sale is pitched makes all the difference in the world. If the method works on these infomercials, then you must know that it works on the basic psyche of all consumers. If you haven't figured it out yet, then let me help you. When it comes to infomercials it's not the quality of the product that matters; it is the quality of the marketing. Even if these companies give you a money-back guarantee, they know you'll not spend the money to ship it back. Before they sell anything, they see whether or not they can build a great marketing package around it. They are actually selling you on the selling of the product. Cool, huh?

You must know that presentation is everything, and it really does matter how you tell people things. It does matter *when* you tell them, and it also matters *where* you tell them. I learned something important a long time ago that has protected me from a lot of grief. Just because I have the right to do something because of my position doesn't mean it is right for me to do it. Did you get that? For every action there is an opposite reaction. The bottom line is that as a leader you must study well each situation before you react so as not to cause a greater problem than what you have at hand. For example, why are things worse at night? For the most part we are programmed to believe that. So then anything we say or do at night is going to have a totally different affect during the day. It is a simple illustration but nevertheless a true one.

I remember sitting with a mentor who was teaching me about the power of truth. It was then that I also learned the power of the **perception of truth.** I wrote in my notebook, "Truth vs. the Perception of Truth." In either case you have to deal with what is at hand. We must never stray from truthfulness, but we can never ignore one's perception of the truth. It is here that we must navigate through these different perceptions until we lead them safely to real truth. For whatever reason perception is reality and reality to an individual is truth. You will quickly learn that the presentation of information is affected by perception. Perception is affected by where and what time of day you are giving it. It matters what kind of relationship you have with the individual you're giving the information to.

You must take all of these things into account when you as a leader are dealing with important or sensitive information. The delivery of this information doesn't always have to end in chaos. Often we are able to blame our spontaneous reactions back on our positions. After all we are the ones who have to make all of the tough decisions. Now, we cannot use that as an excuse. A little planning and consideration will go a very long way. If something is important enough for you as the leader to be handling it, then it deserves a great deal of thought and effort to make sure it turns out well. Your position will never allow you to ignore consequences under any circumstances. Bad judgment is not a character flaw you want to be known for. Think it through, it's that important.

A Ticket to the Parade

I remember hearing the story of a young boy who lived on a farm outside of town. One day while going into town, he saw a poster on a gate that advertised a circus that was coming to that town. At the bottom of the poster, it said, "Tickets for sale for one dollar!" The boy was so taken by the colorful poster that he pleaded with his father to let him buy a ticket to attend the circus. His father agreed, but only if he would do extra chores which meant getting up earlier in the morning to complete everything. This certainly was not a problem for the boy.

The young boy worked tirelessly to finish the projects his father had given to him. Finally, the time had arrived. As he woke this special day, it was time to get ready for the circus. He finished the last of his chores, gave his father a hug, and took off running toward town. It was a beautiful day and perfect for a circus he thought. As he drew closer to the town, he heard music. The sound of the band only made him run faster. The boy made it to the street and thought it was even more amazing than he imagined. The marching band passed by, followed by the men on stilts. They must have been ten feet tall he thought. And the elephants, could they really be that big? He laughed at the clowns as they clumsily fell and ran into things. The trapeze artists reminded him of the swing down by the creek. There were all kinds of strange animals in big cages. It all was so amazing to him. This was a great show he thought and worth all of the hard work he had done! He was anxious to give his dollar to someone. He saw a man in a bright red coat, wearing a tall black hat. The boy thought surely this man was in charge. As the man passed by, the boy ran to the street and handed him his dollar. "Thank you," he said and then ran home with a smile as wide as his shoulders.

You probably think *what a great story*. But it is not a great story; it is a sad story. You see, what the boy didn't realize was that this was only the parade. It was free and was just a taste of what was to come. He missed the greatest show on earth!

It is so important to stay focused on the main event. It is easy to get people worked up over the plans and all of the hoopla. Being a leader is not just about being a great salesperson; it's about being a great architect and a great builder. But if you do not keep the vision in front of people at all times, you and they will miss the main event. There is nothing more discouraging than to have the hype turn out better than the project. You may have delivered a great marketing pitch, but you will not be going any further. Remember that time is a precious and valuable commodity. Don't abuse the talent that is around you. Nurture and grow it, because in doing so, you grow you.

Jacko the Baboon

Some years ago, a friend of mine told me an interesting story about his boyhood encounters with a baboon while growing up in South Africa. I'll tell you the story as I remember hearing it. I believe that this story is going to help you in a big way. My friend Don talked about how he and his friends were constantly being educated about the dangers and pitfalls that came with the territory of their daily life. One particular event that took place was the intrusive interruption by Jacko the baboon who plagued Don and his companions every morning on their way to school. He explained how this baboon would lie in wait for them as they passed by a particular spot in the road. As they approached the area, Jacko would jump out at them screaming and carrying on as though he were rabid. Don said that all of the kids would throw their lunch sacks at him and then run away giving him exactly what he wanted. Well, it didn't take long for Don's father to figure something out because of his son's huge appetite when he would get home. Don had a dilemma. He wanted the baboon to stop stealing his lunch, but he didn't want anyone to get hurt either. Eventually, his father got the story out of him. Don's father, being the good man that he was, told Don he wasn't going to hurt the baboon but knew exactly how to catch him.

The weekend came, and they decided it would be the perfect opportunity to beat Jacko at his own game. Don was so surprised when he saw the trap that his father had prepared for Jacko. In fact it almost seemed as though they were going to be rewarding the baboon for what he was doing. The trap was a jar full of treats that was attached to the ground. Don asked his father how that was going to work because the baboon could just reach in and take the treats out. Don's father said that would be true if Jacko wasn't so greedy. Don asked his father what he meant, and he told him to watch and learn a valuable lesson.

Well, it didn't take Jacko long to notice the activity, and he was soon making his way toward the place in the road. Don's father had Don walk toward the jar so that Jacko would want to take it from him. It worked, and Jacko sprang into action! He came in screaming and waving his arms, and Don took off running. Don's father grabbed him as he ran by and told him to watch. Jacko reached into the small opening of the jar and grabbed a huge handful of the treats. But when he tried to pull his hand out, it wouldn't fit through the top of the jar. All Jacko had to do was open his hand and let the treats go, and he would be free, but he would not let them go. Don's father and a couple of men just walked up and threw a net over Jacko and carried him to a secluded part of the jungle to set him free. It could have cost Jacko his life.*

I guess by now you know the moral of the story. Let it go. Whatever you're trying to hang onto isn't worth the price it is going to cost you. Sometimes leaders feel that having control is having their hands on everything that takes place. Nothing could be further from the truth! If you're a great leader, then you surely are raising great leaders under you. So let go and watch the talent soar. That's what great leaders do, remember? They empower those around them.

A side note that may help you, this application works well for moral conduct also. Step back and measure the cost before you make a decision that could wind up costing you more than you were prepared to pay. It's not worth it; let it go!

*Jacko the Baboon is a children's book written by Don Normand.

Life Application Review

Section Two

Are you really serious about what you're doing? Well, then, don't let the fact that there are no resources around be the excuse for not doing something. If you can't find what you need, then create the tools to get it done. That's what a true leader does. Leading means you are getting others to a certain destination. If there is a desire to get there, then there has to be a way to make it happen. Some can look at obstacles and use them as an excuse while others look at them and see opportunities. It is up to you. By the way, there are some really great excuses out there.

It doesn't matter what you think, presentation is everything. Until you have learned this truth, you will never be ready to lead. There are always right places and right times under right circumstances to do all things. How you say things in all situations will spell success or disaster. Timing is of the utmost importance as well. Just because you are in a position of authority and have the right to say something doesn't mean you should. You are a leader so that you can empower others as well. You are the one who has to make the tough decisions, so why complicate them even more? Think the presentation and timing through!

Don't ever settle for the parade. There have been more celebrations along with time and money spent on plans than on actual accomplishments. You can never celebrate winning a race before the gun's been fired. All you do is eat the fruits of potential and never taste of true victory. If all you do is spend your time getting revved up you find out very soon that you've gone nowhere. Your team suffers the loss because they have already celebrated until there is nothing left to celebrate. Don't use the hype as the motivation. Cast the vision.

When they get it, you won't be able to hold them back. Make it count, every time.

Control is not all it's cut out to be. Being in charge doesn't mean you have to control everything. Manage your people well. If you are leading them properly, then they are taking on your attributes. They are growing as leaders themselves and operate in the scope of your influence. If you cannot have confidence in your own leadership, then what are you doing there? You should step to the back of the line until you see that you have what it takes to lead. Insecurities and rejection issues will cause you to self-destruct. Get them dealt with so that there is no collateral damage.

As a leader you will have certain opportunities afforded you that are not always in your best interests. Your character should be the guardian of your decision making. You may often think that the grass is greener on the other side. It may appear that way, but greener grass also needs a lot more mowing. We are seldom prepared to pay the price that some decisions cost us. Let go of those things that are not going to make you a better leader and grab hold of the future; you're not missing that much.

Section Three

Have I Told You Lately That I Love You?

This information is going to be the opposite of what you think. If there is a phrase that has been used and abused and tossed around like an old rag, it's the phrase, "I love you, man." You know what? Just stop it, please! You don't mean it, so why use it? It's true, and you know it. You just thought of someone who says that to you all the time, and you know for a fact they don't mean it. So don't do it yourself.

The words *I love you* should be reserved for those we are in association with on a level that goes far beyond the workplace. These words are particularly abused by guys. Women know the power of those words and do not toss them around lightly. In fact most wives would give anything to have their husbands say those words to them—as they so easily say the words to their friends—and really mean them!

Actions really do speak louder than words. You will always find time for what you are really passionate about, no matter what the circumstances. I could spend a short time with you and know what moves you most. It's a fact. Most of the people around you probably see the same things. A much better application of expression would be to tell someone that you appreciate them for being a part of the team, make sure they know how much talent they bring to the table, and then reinforce your words with action. Whether with bonuses, incentives, or recognition, backing your appreciation with demonstration means a lot more than empty words. End a telephone conversation with something like, "I really do appreciate your friendship, and I'm glad you're a part of the team." That along with your actions takes your influence to a whole new level.

Have you ever been talking with someone whose eyes filled with tears as they were telling you about something they were going through? You can't see that in an e-mail or text message. Technology is an amazing thing, but it has separated us from the personal touch of communication. We say things we probably shouldn't because we can avoid the consequences of what words do to us as well as others. As a leader take time to have face-to-face conversations with those around you, and you will see a much more supportive team that's chasing the vision with you. You need it as much as they do; reach out and touch someone.

Know When to Exit the Wave

Growing up around the Florida beaches gives one a whole different perspective of water. This is especially true when it comes to waves and in particular riding them. It seemed that just about everyone in school at one time or another surfed or had a brother or sister who surfed. Cocoa Beach used to host some really big East Coast surfing contests. Surfers from around the country would come in to compete. Like every other sport, there is a great deal of skill required to compete on a professional scale. One thing that was critical to the surfers was to know when to exit the waves.

Let me explain. Surfers were allotted a certain number of waves to ride in a short time period. They had to sit out there and watch for the perfect wave to build, and (to complicate things) they had to beat the competition to it. They had to work the wave as much as possible, scoring points for the different maneuvers that showed their skills. The key was to work the wave during its greatest strength but to also get off of it when it was collapsing or blowing out. You could still ride the wave when it collapsed, but it was taking you farther from the bigger waves and closer to shore, which was the opposite of where you wanted to be. So the object was to catch the biggest wave, work it, and get off to position yourself for the next one.

As a leader you are constantly creating and casting vision. Remember that the vision creates the provision. Use what works and work it until it's time to release it. Don't get comfortable with what works simply because you're used to it. Get off of the wave because there is a bigger, more powerful wave swelling behind you, and you will miss it if you keep pumping the one you're riding. The same old methods and practices will ultimately take you all the way to shore.

The worst place to be is standing on the beach while everyone else is riding the big one.

Everything has a season, and sometimes you like an idea so much that you are not willing to adjust or improve on it for sentimental reasons. Maybe you just feel safe with it. You always have to stay focused on the bigger picture. Know your plan and then work the plan. Listen to those around you, and you will know when to move on. There is something bigger swelling up behind you. There will always be risk, but if you are willing to be objective and aggressive with new concepts, then you will come out on top. Remember that safe isn't always the best place to be.

I Thought You Turned
the Gas Off!

I had a friend tell me one time about a brain hiccup he had in his early years. He said he loved to grill in the spring. He and his wife would do all of their cooking on that grill, and this was no ordinary grill. It was a six-burner stainless steel grill with a thermostat, a warmer, and two side burners. Now, it was a really nice grill, but it had one little flaw: a leaking control valve. He always had to make sure to turn the gas off. One afternoon he had finished cooking, and his wife, as she always had done, reminded him to shut the gas off. The pan he was holding was hot, so he ran inside with it and told his wife to go and shut the gas off. Now, remember that she too is busy getting ready for the meal. A short time into the meal, he remembered the gas and asked his wife if she remembered to shut the gas off. She responded by telling him it was his responsibility to do that. He went out back, smelled a hint of gas, and then did something that lowered his IQ a few numbers. He took out his lighter to see if there was gas leaking. And guess what? Right, he blew the lid off the grill. He was lucky he wasn't killed! You know what happened after that, right? An argument ensued which really solved nothing. The grill was damaged and arguing wasn't going to fix it.

I remember a time, while under good leadership, when I was held accountable for those things that didn't get done under my watch. The organization had a large staff, and we had weekly staff meetings. We used a term at those meetings called "dropping the ball." It was applied to those things that didn't get done. One of the staff members decided to make it more interesting, so he brought in a can of Grip Spray. It was a sticky spray that athletes use on their hands to make the ball stick when they attempt to catch it. Whoever had dropped the most balls that week would be awarded the can at the staff meeting. Being awarded the can was not a good thing. The important thing I learned was that making excuses for not doing something I was responsible for made me a weaker leader. The idea was to cover the bases and when things didn't get done, own up to the failure and make sure it didn't happen again.

Delegation only works if there has been successful communication. Remember that communication is the sharing of information that has been comprehended, otherwise it's just chatter. Accept the responsibility for the results. If you did not make sure that you gave clear, detailed instructions that were discussed and understood, then you own the blame. Blaming someone else to protect your own leadership can cause you to kick yourself in the rear. I don't think we can fully grasp the damage we do to those we throw under the bus because we as leaders want to protect ourselves. It really isn't that complicated. Cover your bases, review your checklist, and make sure everyone has a clear understanding of his/her responsibilities. Inspect the process; be the cheerleader. You are ultimately responsible for the results anyway. If something doesn't go right, accept the responsibility for it. Learn from the situation and move on to complete the project. You are the leader, remember?

Let the Rough Edges Drag

If you have spent any time in the South at all, you have probably heard this cliché before. A friend and I were visiting in Alabama on some business. We had stopped to talk to a particular gentleman about a business he was selling. I remember my partner asking about some of the details involving the tracking of expenses as well as the checks and balances that were in place for the business. He looked at us for a second and then said, ***"Awe, we just throw it all in the back of the truck and let the rough edges drag."***

This man simply meant that they just didn't worry about those kinds of details. The phrase was related to the process of working with lumber. Sometimes the edges of lumber shipments are damaged when they're picked up, but the rest of the lumber is good. The rough edges of the wood are going to be cut off anyway, so there's no need to worry if the rough edges are hanging off the back of the truck. So basically don't worry about it; it will all work out. Trust me; the concept of "Don't worry about it," only works out if somebody is working it out. Don't forget it!

As a leader you will come to respect the other cliché you may have heard as well. It is, "The small fox spoils the vine." This is without question an absolute truth. The small things will always be those that get you down and here's the reason. They're never singular. These little problems always travel in packs. When they happen, they happen all over the place. The small things may not seem like that big of a deal and ignoring them may seem to be the best thing to do. Wrong! What you don't anticipate is their timing. They show up just after the big problem arrives. And all these little things become the final straw!

Now, there is no way to prevent every small problem from happening, but you will have the opportunity to see them coming and to develop a strategy to deal with them. Listen to your staff. Go over possible fallout situations. Discuss how to communicate through departments and find solutions. It doesn't mean that you personally have to chase these things down. You shouldn't have the time, but you had better have someone in place that does. If you don't, when you get to your destination, you may find that those rough edges got snagged on something, and the lumber you were going to use on your new project was ripped right from the back of the truck. Try to take care of as many of the small issues as you can while you have the time, and the bigger ones may be fewer and farther between. Nothing ever just works out unless someone is working it out.

Life Application Review

Section Three

There is nothing more irritating than the use of words that are empty of true feeling. The words "I love you, man" are some of those words. So often you get used to saying things out of habit, and you don't know the impact they're having on the people around you. There are leaders who have adopted that phrase and have wielded it like a six-shooter, pointing it at anyone within sight. I would prefer a celebration of my performance in genuine expression rather than to hear misplaced words that are not sincere. When you are talking to your team, those "I love you, man" words are not necessary. You will get far more mileage from public recognitions of jobs well done. Celebrate the wins with the team, and you will have no problem communicating to your team how much you appreciate what they bring to the table.

It is human nature to stick with what you know. For example, I know people who have been handed the opportunity of a lifetime and have watched them let it go because it was something foreign to them. New and untested opportunities come along all of the time, but being there to seize them is the key. You have to be willing to stretch yourselves far beyond what you thought possible. Something may be good right now, but something greater may be around the corner. That means you have to be willing to let go of what you're holding in order to grab what is coming. There is no guarantee that what you have will be what is wanted tomorrow.

Great leaders are forged from great character. If you are going to be a great leader, then you must be willing to accept responsibility. The buck does stop with you. There will be so many opportunities to blame others for failure in any given circumstance. Remember that all who are under you are striving to help your vision come to pass and have bought into the overall plan. The plan is not a you-thing and a them-thing. It is a team-thing that requires someone to stand up and take charge, and that means you've got to accept responsibility when others fall short.

Stay out of the weeds. Distractions are probably the leading cause of failure. Many great plans have never come to pass because of distractions. They come from everywhere and usually seize the opportunity to strike at the worst possible moments. These distractions shift the focus, and the valuable time allotted for the project is spent on sifting through the weeds. Pick your concerns and have responsible team members track down those stray problems. Examine what needs to be attended to and correct the problems. Don't let small issues build until they become real problems. You will learn in time that if you stay focused, you will not only see greater advances, you will feel healthier for it. And remember. Nothing just works out. Things happen because someone, somewhere makes them happen.

Section Four

Who in the #@!!* Are You?

Leading is about relationships! That is one of the most powerful truths I have learned in leadership. Many great leaders have said that rules without relationships breed rebellion. And you know what? It's the truth! There are countless leaders who constantly push their people to perform the impossible tasks and don't understand why they complain and why their performance levels drop. Every leader would like to think that he/she is loved by all because, "Well, it's me, man; I'm the one in charge!" That's usually how a boss thinks. The only person you can count on to love you because you're you, might be a parent—maybe.

When I worked with kids in the inner city, I experienced a tremendous time of growth. I thought that if these kids saw me down at the center every day, I would be able to convince them that I was there for them. I didn't. They thought I was there because it was my job to be there. One day while on my way to the center, I saw a fight at the corner of the street beside our facility. I recognized some of the kids and called for them to come over to me. They looked over and motioned for me to get lost. I knew that's what they were communicating because of the particular sign language they used with one of their fingers.

Over time, situations arose that warranted my going to their homes to help them through difficult times, like the loss of a loved one. I would take groceries and fix bicycles and toys, doors and windows. I even threw out some unruly guests. It was then I realized that something was happening. We were building relationships. Now when I called to the kids from across the street, they came running. You see, I had to earn the right to speak into their lives. **I EARNED THE RIGHT!**

Respect is not something you demand; it's something that is given to you. What an incredible privilege to have someone offer respect to you. Don't abuse your position because you have the power to do so; earn respect by getting to know the people who are making it happen for you. Listen, I understand that you may be in charge of a lot of people, but you can start with the ones over whom you have direct influence. Maybe you could even start with your family. You can effect life change in someone. Why not start with those who provide you the opportunity for it every day? Give them something powerful to follow. Show them they have a leader who cares.

Try Before You Pry

While attending the Florida State Fire College, my fellow fire-fighters and I learned just about everything we could about how fire works. We learned about something called the Fire Tetrahedron or Fire Triangle. The three legs of the triangle represented the components that made fire. They were heat, oxygen, and fuel. If you were to remove any one of those legs, the fire would go out. By knowing how a fire worked, we then knew how to extinguish it. It was intense training, and we learned a lot of important information to keep us alive. Even with that training, however, there were some practical things that we overlooked because we had the power to overlook them. In fact, I've seen cartoons depicting some of those practical applications.

Let me tell you about a practical application that was overlooked during one of our shifts. Because of the shortage of man power actually on shift at the fire station, we often looked to volunteers to help respond to structural fires. I remember pulling up to a particularly large house with huge double front doors on it. There was a little smoke coming from the end of the roof. As we started to put our breathing gear on for search and rescue, we heard all kinds of chopping and banging noises. Some of the new volunteers had arrived before us and had started to chop at those big, solid doors. Our lieutenant walked up and asked the guys how it was going. They told LT that the doors were tougher than they thought. He looked at them and asked if they'd tried turning the knob, because sometimes people forget to lock their doors. He reached up and turned the handle, and the door opened right up. The problem turned out to be an attic fan that had overheated and was smoking. The situation could have been disastrous, but in this case we arrived in time to prevent further damage. It turned out that the damage to the doors was the only real expense.

As a leader you will constantly be in situations that will warrant immediate attention. Remember that there are always various ways to go about your decision making. Just because you have the power and the tools to cut through or blow the doors off doesn't mean the situation warrants that action. You may actually cause more damage by crashing through apparent barriers than the actual problem would have caused. Step back and assess the situation. You already know what you're capable of. Gather all of the information you can. Try all the options you have that will cause the least amount of damage and if all these avenues fail, then you know you have no other choice. Damage control is a key factor to great leadership, and there is nothing more helpful than preventive measures. They're cheaper.

The Word for the Day
Is *Retention!*

A great leader will make sure that he/she always stays true to their standard. It is a character thing again. You will go no further than your character will take you because you can never lead where you've never been. If you're taking people some place that you've never been before, then you're not leading them. You just happen to be at the front of the line. Remember that preparation precedes promotion. If you've never been to your destination, you haven't been able to prepare yourself or anyone else to seize the moment, so what makes you different from the rest of the group?

Some time ago, I had the good fortune of working with a close friend on a construction project. His brother-in-law was the contractor and had invited us to help him out. It was a unique experience, as he would set us down every day before we started and would give to us the word for the day. Something you would expect from a Marine veteran. Anyway, sometimes the word would have to do with safety or pride in your work, but this particular day it was *retention*. I love one particular definition of retention: "the preservation of the aftereffects of experience" (Merriam-Webster). It is perfect for what we're talking about.

The day started out great! We were busy working on our assigned tasks for the morning. My particular task was to cut all of the roof trusses for the small addition to the back of the house. The contractor told me to measure each piece of lumber to a particular length, cut the pieces, and then place them where they would be hung. I remembered him saying to me, "Measure twice and cut once." But hey, come on now. It's about time, right? So I thought to myself, *I may not have the skills or the schooling or even the experience that he has, but I can have a better idea then he does*, right? Wrong! Think about what I just said! I just wanted to do something my way. So instead of measuring each piece of lumber, I would cut a piece and use it to measure my next piece of wood. And I did this to every piece I cut. Well, as we broke for lunch I was called over to the cutting area. The contractor asked me if I remembered the word for the day. I said I certainly did. It was *retention*. He then asked me what happened. I asked him what he meant. He then showed me the lumber laying out on the ground. To my shock each piece was a little longer than the one next to it. He had me show him step by step what I had done to complete the task. Instead of measuring each piece, I had used the piece I had just cut as a jig. He laughed and said that I left out one important detail: the width of the saw blade. It was one-eighth of an inch thick. By using the previously cut wood, I was adding an eighth of an inch to each new piece. The good news was we could still use the wood; the bad news was we lost an entire morning because of my better idea.

You see, what happened was I didn't follow instructions and strayed from the true standard, which was the tape measure. The numbers would never change, so it would not have failed me. I failed the crew and myself. In life, though, there are seldom small casualties. If we do not hold ourselves to a high standard and then remain true to those standards, we have nowhere to bring anyone. We spend most of our time trying to correct mistakes. Remember that not all mistakes are correctable, and most of the time you have to start over from the beginning. Don't be a leader who gets tired of holding the line and looks for shortcuts. Over time, one-eighth of an inch turns into feet and then yards, and, well, you know. Remain true to your convictions, and if you have none, find some because you will need them to take others where they need to go. Remember to measure twice and cut only once.

Recalculating

Had I used this word a few years ago, you probably wouldn't have known where I'm going with this. It would seem that before long just about everyone is going to have a GPS in his or her phone as well as their vehicle. What they can do is certainly amazing. You can find anything by using a GPS. While you drive, the system alerts you to turns and street locations. If you would like it to do so, the GPS will give you alternate routes to avoid traffic; they are quite useful systems.

When using your GPS, you will become very familiar with one word in particular. That word is *recalculating*. There are times that you will program a destination into the GPS, and then you will decide to take a different road than the system mapped out. It will immediately notify you that it is recalculating your navigational routes to put you back on course to reach your destination. The best part about it is that it doesn't get on your case about what happened. It just methodically tries to get you back on track.

As a leader there will be times and situations that will cause you to take a detour. You may end up in uncharted territories, and the road may not even be stored in your GPS. At these times you have to recalculate. Course calculations that GPS units use are based on triangulations. You have a starting point, a destination, and a point of reference. Sometimes the point of reference can be the most important piece of information. It tells you where you are and whether or not you need to make adjustments to your course. You are en route to a destination. You have a dream that you are in pursuit of. You are reading this information because you want to learn. There will be bumps and detours in the road. You will have options and decisions to make. Do you take heed to the warning to readjust your course or do you just throw caution to the wind? Like many, you may say I don't want to go back there and start over. You may not have it in you to go back down that same road again. C. S. Lewis said that if you're on the wrong road then going back was actually progress if it was going to put you on the right road. Either way, you have to decide whether it is worth it or not. Only you can define what your passion is!

Leadership is about knowing how to navigate. Others are trusting in you to empower them with your knowledge. There will come a time when they will hear the word *recalculating*. They will also have to make a decision. Do they abort the journey, or do they find a reference point and readjust their positioning so that they can get back on track to finish the journey?

The influences that are around you help keep you focused on the task at hand. There is nothing as powerful as the responsibility of influence. How are you going to use it? Choose to be the reference point. It is such an honorable position. People always know where they are starting from and most know the destination but few know how to get there. They stray and lose hope. What they need is a reference point to show them the way so they might recalculate from where they're at. As a leader I can't think of more reliable reference points than great character and passion. Do you know where you are?

Life Application Review

Section Four

I do not believe you will find a more solid truth today than the one that says you have to earn the right to speak into people's lives. Mere position does not cut it. People usually don't have a problem following rules. What they have a problem with is someone who discards relationship without regard to individualism. Granted, it is the workplace, and people are supposed to be doing their jobs; you most certainly shouldn't have to sweet-talk anyone. But remember that you're not just their boss; you're their leader. There is nothing more powerful than having a team that has you as their captain. This means the team recognizes you as the go-to person. This is where you want to be.

If you push people and abuse them because you are the boss, then you will accomplish two things: insubordination and a bad nickname, not to mention poor work productivity. So before you rush in expecting everyone to follow you, get to know the people who are going to make you successful. If they get it and feel that you are for them as much as for the vision, then you will have no problem setting goals high because you will be taking them with you.

Remember that the situation may seem chaotic, but your thoughtless reaction to it may be catastrophic. This doesn't mean the situation does not require immediate attention. It simply means that there is a right move that is best suited for the problem. If you have time to step back to gather your thoughts or maybe even call for some support, you might be surprised at how well the situation comes off.

Set your mark high and remain true to your standard. There will be lots of situations that cry out for compromise but remember to stay with your original measuring point and demand that everything else come up to that standard. Soon everyone you know will be trying to bring their levels up to meet yours.

If you're on a journey to somewhere, then you are going to want a good navigator. This is what great leadership is all about. If you can navigate well and negotiate through unexpected difficulties, then everyone will want to follow you. Again, most of us know where we're starting from and know where we want to go, but we don't really know where we are. You find your true path from triangulation, and if you know all three points, then you will remain on course. Remember, you are in route to a destination, if you are off course then recalculate and put your steps in order. Don't place blame or make excuses as this will only put you in places you would never have desired to be. Everybody is going somewhere; most just never get there.

Section Five

A Bird in the Hand

Procrastination is terminal! Not only is it expensive, it's highly destructive. As a leader it is your responsibility to lead by example when it comes to the execution of deadlines. In order to do this, you not only need a great team to assist you, but you need to be diligent to monitor your progress. If you don't have a plan for everything, then remember that everything will have a plan for you, and it will come to you at all of the wrong times.

When my boys were young, they were constantly on a mission into the woods just behind our home. They would build forts, fend off the imaginary bad guys, and explore strange new worlds. There was, however, one particular time when they brought me into one of their intense ventures. They had found a couple of bird feathers underneath the back deck of the house. They decided to follow the feathers that ultimately led them to a small dove underneath the steps. They came running into the house yelling for me to assist them. As I met the boys at the backdoor, they told me of their discovery. My reaction was less than enthusiastic to say the least. It was winter in New England and almost dark to boot! But then I had a "paragon of introspection" (great idea). I told the boys that doves nest on the ground sometimes, which they do, and that he would be fine there in the warmth of the steps by the house. They seemed content with my response and felt I would not steer them down the wrong path. They thanked me and ran off to play.

Early the next morning, I remembered the dove crisis and figured that I should go and make sure that the dove was okay. I knew that would be the first place they would be headed when they got up. I made my way downstairs, opened the backdoor, and to my horror saw feathers everywhere. Within a few seconds I knew what had happened. I threw some gloves on and began to pick up the feathers before the boys came outside. As I was making my way up the back steps, I saw the neighbor's cat sitting there licking its paws. If the cat could have talked, he would have thanked me for such a fine meal. I actually had no one to blame but myself.

I went back inside, and after a short while, the boys made their way outside and came in and told me I was right; the bird was gone. All I could think of was, *He's gone all right!* I let them down because I procrastinated. When I first saw that bird, I told myself, *He's lunch for a cat if he stays down there.* But then I made excuses and explained it away: *How would that cat even know he's down there? It's cold out,* and on and on I went.

What's important to remember is that my boys trusted me. My gut told me I needed to act. There is no comparison that can be made between the value of that bird and the value of an individual. What we do not understand is that our procrastination is putting people in jeopardy somehow. We cause more pressure and stress when we put them in unhealthy environments. It's just not healthy for anyone to be subjected to another's constant procrastination. I urge you as a leader to cast vision, delegate, delineate, and work the plan. Monitor your progress and make sure that you communicate with everyone the importance of taking care of business. Everyone will prosper from it. You know what you're supposed to do. Do it!

Absitively-Posilutely

    I don't believe there is anything more settling than a confident leader. Confidence makes them so much easier to follow. At the same time, however, there is nothing more discouraging than an arrogant leader. The differences between the two are as broad as the Grand Canyon. Confidence is a reflection of who the leader is whereas arrogance is a reflection of who a leader thinks he/she is. It's all about character. Without character you will not be able to take your leadership skills very far. A confident person has done their homework and is applying personal knowledge to empower others. An arrogant leader has focused only on themselves while coping with personal issues of rejection and abandonment. Arrogant leaders will always surface because they are self-destructive. The real tragedy in this is that their destruction produces collateral damage as well. But it is no big deal to them because they are focused on themselves, the constant victim.

    Most people recognize the arrogant leader because he/she is also a pretender and pretending only works temporarily. When real-life situations occur, pretending just doesn't cut it. On the other hand, what makes us so attracted to the confident leader? It's simple; we are followers. I often tell young leaders that it is amazing how easy it is to gain control of a group of people. I use the example that I could be in a grocery store and if the power were to go off, I could be in control in a matter of seconds. All I would have to do is grab a flashlight, jump up on the checkout table, and say, "May I have everyone's attention, please?" At that moment everyone would move toward the light. Once I assured them that everything was going to be okay, I could then give the group the instructions that I wanted them to follow.

    As soon as most people enter the unknown, they need leadership. They find comfort in following. They have to have someone to follow because they don't trust their own decision making abilities. They need to know that someone knows what to do. A leader's confidence informs everyone that he/she has a plan and is the right one in charge. They then become the one everyone else should follow. Arrogance alerts everyone to look at the leader as the only one that's important and needs no help from others. He/she is the leader, and they are not. People tire of the arrogant pretender very quickly. Unfortunately, a lot of people are dependent upon their jobs and don't have the power to do anything about working for an arrogant pretender unless they are prepared to walk away from their livelihoods. But what ever you do, don't become one of them.

As a leader you have the incredible opportunity to empower others to reach their full potential. Ultimately, you have a direct effect on the quality of life for many. Leadership is an amazing responsibility to have and not many recognize this. What about you? What do you see in the mirror every morning? I trust that you see someone who has done their research, someone who has learned well the jobs of those for whom they are responsible, that they may lead them to high places. If this is you, then congratulations and thank you for the sacrifices and tough calls you will have to make on the behalf of others. Confidence definitely looks good on you!

Are You Hurt or Injured?

There is nothing more tragic than to see someone with so much potential miss their future. Everyone who has walked this earth has been subject to hurt in one way or another. How deep the hurt goes will decide who continues forward and who sits it out. I was watching a football movie a while back. The team was practicing, and as the running back went through the line of players, someone hit him so hard he fumbled and was lying on the ground stunned. The coach ran up to him and asked him as he lay there if he was hurt or injured? The player told the coach that he didn't understand what he meant. The coach said, "Well, if you are injured, then you couldn't play anymore, but if you are just hurt, then get up off the ground and get back into the huddle."

As a leader this is an assessment you will have to make constantly. Situations and circumstances, whether personal or public, will hit you at the times you least expect them, and you will end up on your back gasping for air. You might have even fumbled the ball of life. It is there when you're looking up at the heavens that you will have to decide what your condition is. I remember one time, while I was going through a difficult situation; a friend reminded me that life throws you curves sometimes. I immediately responded back to him. I told him I used to play baseball and that I knew how to hit a curve, it was life's bean ball that I was worried about. You can hit a curve over the fence. Worst-case scenario, it brushes you back away from the plate. But a bean ball can take you out of the game possibly forever. So in essence there is a big difference.

While working with the kids in the inner city, I developed a creed that we taught the kids every week. It went like this: "**Losing to a better opponent may make you a better competitor; but losing to**

you is unacceptable. Never, ever quit on you!" You can live with the fact that someone prepared better than you did and maybe he/she was just a little better than you were. You have the ability to get better. But when you quit and you quit on yourself, you will forever be reminded that you made the decision to quit. You beat yourself, and there is no way to ever know how far you could have gone.

Oh, there will be plenty of excuses along the way to justify quitting. And in some circumstances no one would blame you and would probably do the same if they were in your shoes as well. But you still will be the one making the choice. Trust me. There will always be opportunities to quit, but there are very few windows of opportunity to succeed. Don't let the blows that come from life keep you down. If you are injured, then you have no choice but to leave the game. You will find a way to succeed in another arena. But if you're only hurt, then get your butt up off the ground and get back into the huddle because you've got a game to win!

The Twelve-Foot Shuffle

Some time ago, I listened to a Native American chief tell one of the most powerful stories I've ever heard. The chief told of his childhood growing up in the wilderness and his many encounters with the wildlife living in the forest. He shared how he used to visit a man who trapped for a living. Sometimes the trapper would keep the animals as pets. To his surprise, one day he came up to the place and saw a bear chained to a tree. The trapper warned that even though he was young the bear was dangerous and that he was preparing a cage for him. Over time the boy and his friends would go by and feed the bear. But as they grew older, the bear seemed to weaken, and they felt sorry for it because it lived in a twelve-foot-long cage. They had asked the trapper to free the bear, but he would not; he said it was worth a lot of money.

The passion for the bear's freedom grew and spread throughout the area. Finally, with all of the attention brought to the bear's plight, the people raised the money to buy the bear's freedom. To celebrate, the people brought food and prepared games for this festive occasion. When the time finally came to release the bear, everyone gathered to witness this big event. A great roar came from the crowd as the trapper opened the end of the cage. The bear made his way to the opening, the crowd applauded but then silence fell as the bear stopped at the opening. He just stared, and then turned to walk back to the other end. The trapper thought maybe he was frightened of the opening and decided to pull all of the pins so that the cage fell flat. The crowd's roar again grew as the bear began to move but then again silence followed. The bear walked twelve feet then stopped and turned back. Saddened and in disbelief the people stood watching. The trapper reassembled the cage and declared that the bear knew nothing else but the twelve-foot area of this cage. He had refused the very thing his instinct longed for, freedom. That bear died in that cage secure in his bondage and safe from the fear of change.

What will it take for you as leader to take the next step that will bring change? It is easy to stay in your comfort zone, even if it is killing you. And what of those who are looking to you for direction? Will you know how to lead them out even when they say they are afraid to do something different? Remember the old cliché that says, "If nothing changes then nothing changes." A leader has to be able to make the hard decisions and to cast vision so that others will be willing to take the steps toward change. If you know this going into a leadership role, then you can begin to build your support to embrace the newness of change. Be that leader who will see the potential in others and empower them to take the next step to greater things than they've ever imagined, to things they only dreamed of. It all begins with one more step. Get out of the cage!

Life Application Review

Section Five

Once again, I cannot overemphasize the danger of procrastination. This bad habit will rob you of more victories than you thought possible. It is important always to step back and thoroughly examine your situations, but do not mistake caution for lethargy. There are windows of opportunity that are opening up around you at critical times. You have to do everything within your power to make sure you are in a position to capitalize on them. Situations and events will come up at the worst possible times, and you will certainly have access to plenty of excuses, but you must press through. Find that drive inside of you and seize that opportunity.

Confidence is a powerful as well as a very settling attribute. Arrogance, however, is a turnoff. You will never be a great leader without confidence. You will have to be sure of your gifting and your ability to make right decisions at a moment's notice. Notice I said the *right* decision instead of the *popular* decision. You will always have the opportunity to abuse power and let arrogance move in. Arrogance is like a cancer that will eat away at a great leader's potential. You must always stay focused on the team and remember that your success is really based on the overall success of the team. A simpleton can make money and brag on themselves, but only a true leader can empower others. Do the right thing!

Whether you choose to accept it or not, your leadership will always have some characteristics based on your past. A number of things could have taken place, but you must step back and determine the extent of your injuries. All of us get shaken up in one way or another. It is when we're down that we need to know whether or not we can get back into the game. There is nothing wrong with being injured; it is a part of life and sometimes it's devastating. You can only do what is in you to do, and then time will be the deciding factor. But if you have only been hurt, then you need to accept it, work through it, and then move on. You cannot live there. Focusing on being hurt will trap you in defeat. It will hold you back from reaching your place as a leader. Don't get comfortable with the hurt. Resist what it is trying to do to you and forge ahead. Take that next critical step to move beyond the bondage to claim new territory. You are far more valuable to yourself and to others to let this thing immobilize you. Get up and get back into the game; you are a leader and there are many who are waiting to follow you to claim your prize.

Section Six

Hey, Coach!

I have often wondered why coaches from college-level positions have such a difficult time transitioning into the professional arena. Most are certainly qualified and have performed with winning records. But it seems that there is a barrier to overcome in order to succeed in the professional venues. I have my own theory, and I will share it with you.

Coaching, for all intents and purposes, is a calling. Let me explain. The art of coaching usually differs greatly from that of managing. To be a coach means you have to be a teacher. If you are teaching, it means that you are working with impressionable minds, and you are developing talent. Basically all of the skills are there, but for the time being they are in the developmental stages. Often a player may think that a certain position is right for him/her, but the coach will see something else that the player might dominate in. Also a coach's responsibility usually takes them beyond the field and into the homes and difficult situations that life throws at their players. Therefore they become more like a surrogate family member. This is very important because all coaches know that the emotional and mental state of their players affects their performance on the field. So the coach must then deal with these issues to move forward in developing the skills of the player.

When players have advanced their skills, they move to the next level and become professionals. Something happens at this level. They have gained control of their skills and now become more creative in their abilities to perform. They move from the instructional phase to the performance phase. For the coach this is very difficult. He/she now takes on more of a management role. If you as a coach cannot make this transition, then you will not succeed. Professionals do not like to be coached concerning their skills. They will, however, let you manage them to their full potential as a team player. A great leader will recognize the talent their employees have and will work to form individual talent into team talent. He/she becomes an encourager and a great leader. A professional knows their trade, and—if given the right tools and the right plays—can perform with winning results.

As a leader you will work both as the coach and the manager. You have to be flexible. If you have young talent, you will recognize their potential quickly and will be able to grow that talent to win. At other times you will be the manager. The talent you are working with has experience and knows how to win. Your job will be to make sure they play as a team and that the right tools are in place to allow them to do what they do best: win!

Who's the Boss?

Write this one down! A boss isn't necessarily a leader. They could just be the one in charge. You might think that this one is a no-brainer, but a lot of people don't see it. Bosses manage companies while leaders empower people. It is the boss who will become procedurally minded and will focus only on tasks. The leader will be goal minded and will measure progress corporately by first measuring it individually. The leader knows success is about the people. If their team is growing individually, they know it is just a matter of time before the operation as a whole begins to see the result. So for the leader, progress begins with each individual. Do they see and get the vision? Are they in the right positions to reach their full potential? Have they been equipped with the right tools and are communication lines open for clear delineation? These are the important things for the leader to know about his team of people.

A boss will go through the list of quotas and will cite the team for failing to perform. The boss is the one who is ultimately responsible but usually does not interact with the team to find out what is going on. This is why they have department heads, right? Wrong. Department heads are in position to reaffirm the vision of the house. I see them more as stabilizers such as you would find on the wings of an aircraft. They help facilitate the smooth operation of the plane. If you only look at department heads as task masters, then you severely cripple the chances of getting to the levels you want to achieve. Not only do you restrict creativity and morale, you separate yourself as the boss from your team.

Most people, as a rule of thumb, do not like what they are doing for a career, yet you as the leader are responsible for the success of their labors. I remember seeing a boss in rare form one time while I was eating at a fast-food place. There were people in line to order as well as some who were seated enjoying their meal. All of the sudden the manager begins to speak loudly. Addressing his employees, he says that if they missed their sales quota again, then he was going to make less money. To make up for it, he stated that he was going to take the money from their paychecks. Everyone was looking at him as he barked out this threat. People in the place were actually calling him names.

That is exactly how a boss acts. These jobs are not career positions for most people. That boss lost his team's loyalty, if he ever had it. What he should have done was to challenge or to offer incentives to the team for meeting their goals. It doesn't take much, either, to inspire additional effort. You can be as creative as you want to be. Fast-food places are great for young people to learn some leadership skills. They learn about customer service, sales and teamwork. Management opportunities are available in a short amount of time as well. Instead of showing great leadership, that boss threw a hand grenade into a situation that needed a sniper rifle. The collateral damage was catastrophic. He hired them all to work for him; he's the one in charge. Who's at fault here?

How do you as the boss become a great leader? First, you have to get it! If you cannot see the prize, then there is no way for you to get anyone else to see it. Second, those who are under the influence of your leadership must be able to feed off of your energy. It really is contagious and will spread until it becomes a part of your very being. And third, leaders create leaders. There are always going to be opportunities to create the atmosphere for leaders to emerge from the ranks. Even in the small things, you can generate creativity that unleashes energy that turns into the passion to succeed. If you can do that, you may even cause those who haven't been happy with their jobs to take a different perspective.

Talented, but Not a Play Maker

While watching the sports channel one night I heard a coach use those words when he was talking about some of his players he was going to have to cut before the football season began. In fact he said of some of the talent that they could be some of the greatest that ever played, but they just couldn't make the big plays. Seems like an oxymoron doesn't it? But it is true nevertheless. Talent is a wonderful gift, but if it is not used, it isn't beneficial to anyone. For some, just the fact that they posses talent is enough, while others would give everything they had to have half of it. So what is the secret to using talent? I believe that it is passion! Passion placed together with talent makes for an unstoppable force.

Passion is the framework that grows talent and giftedness. It is the guardian of talent. Without passion there is no purpose, and without purpose there is no outlet for the talent. Passion is such a powerful force that it can even compensate for the lack of talent. Passion overcomes countless obstacles and is the fuel that drives the will.

Many leaders have so much talent but cannot make the big plays. It is not because they are incapable; it is because they have no passion to use their talent to go beyond the norm. Passion is not something you get; it is something that is stirred up within you. It is the emotion that *compels* one to posses what he/she desires more than anything. It's what pushes you beyond the average to claim the impossible. Passion doesn't mean that you disregard the qualities that make you a great leader; it just means that you want the responsibility of having everyone depend on you. That is a rare quality. There have been some great athletes who have possessed such qualities. You remember Michael Jordan, of course. He felt right at home when everything rested on his shoulders. Even during the championship playoffs, he would ask for the ball knowing it was the final shot of the game. The shot he would take would either win or lose the game. But that's not how he perceived it. He felt that he had the responsibility as a team leader to bring the entire team up to a new level. It built confidence not only for the team, but for him as a team leader.

As leaders today, we are needed more than ever. During difficult times, everyone is looking for someone who will say, "Follow me, we're going to win because I know what to do." Accepting full responsibility for the big plays is what separates those with great potential from those who will make the great plays at just the right time. It is no longer enough just to be talented. True leadership takes the passion to use your talents and to push them to new limits. It is obvious you have the talent, so make the choice to be a playmaker, go ahead and make the shot and take others with you.

Exactly the Same, Just Different

You cannot be a great leader without being a student of who you are leading. Many great leaders will tell you that the best assets of most companies are their employees. Employees equal productivity, profit, and loss. They are the ones who are selling the products and services the company provides. Yet some company leaders look at employees as a liability or an expense. If that happens to be the case, I can almost guarantee you that this particular company is struggling.

Psychologists have determined that there are more than a dozen different personality traits among the human race. This would mean that in every situation involving staff perception, you could end up with as many different views. We as leaders often think that because we explained something, everyone is on the same page. This is not necessarily the case.

I have always been amazed at how difficult it is for leaders to perform evaluations on their staff. In fact most leaders hate it. Why? Could it be that they really don't know their team players? Most likely, this is the reason. If my job is to build a winning team, then you would think that I would want to know where everyone is. I would want to know their abilities and skills. I would want to know what they think of the team and of me as the leader. I would want to know their cultural backgrounds so that I will know best how to communicate information to them. I don't want there to be any weak areas on the team. I didn't just hire anybody to plug a hole. I hired with intentionality to grow the business. And I certainly don't want others to pick up the slack of fellow employees thinking that I expect it of them. That is called workplace abuse.

How does a team exist when I look to certain players to cover the positions of others along with their own? Why would I not take the time to empower those who are struggling? I should be equipping them with the right tools so that they will be playing on the same level as the rest of the team. When I empower the team members with the tools and training they need, I become a great leader. It encourages the team as a whole to know that I care equally about everyone and that, more importantly, I'm not taking advantage of the other team members.

We as leaders must understand that cultural differences affect good communication. Therefore, we must make sure that training methods are working and that information is being understood. We must ensure that the load of work is being equally distributed. By understanding a person's personality, leaders are able to put individuals into the right positions that will better the team. If the team is better, then the leader is better.

We cannot continue without discussing the greatest weakness that all leaders posses, the dreaded stereotyping. You can say you don't do it, but you and I know you do; we all do. We treat people differently based on looks, gender, dress, and even what kind of car they drive. I remember my first job at a large GM dealership down the street from my house. The first thing I had to do when I got there was to wipe down the cars in the showroom. It was also the last thing that I had to do. One night I was wiping down a beautiful 1972 Cadillac Eldorado. It was red with a white convertible top. Back then, it was the top-of-the-line automobile. As I was wiping the thing down, an old pickup truck pulled in and a big, burly farmer type got out. He walked up to me and said, "Now that's a pretty red car." The salesmen were inside watching. He asked me if they were still working, and I told him they were, and that I would go and get one for him. When I stepped inside to tell them that this man was looking at the Eldorado, they laughed and sent the new guy out. To make a long story short, the man was buying the car for his daughter's graduation, and he paid cash for it on the spot. I have never forgotten it, nor will I. Never ever judge a book by its cover. Everyone deserves a fair shake, regardless.

Think about this as a leader. You are in this position to empower people to reach their full potential. The most valuable asset you have is your team of employees. You are daily dealing with situations and circumstances that challenge you to your very core. To add to your responsibilities, you have people from every walk of life who are walking into the workplace. They bring with them personal issues and family issues and financial issues and coworker issues. In the middle of it all, you have production goals to make in order to keep them employed. But this is your team, remember?

Listen. You are not expected to be a psychologist, though it wouldn't necessarily be a bad thing. But you are supposed to know your team. You should look at evaluations as opportunities to be the instructor, the cheerleader, and the mentor. Find a way to impart leadership knowledge that will inspire employees to grow and want to be stronger team players. If you overcome the individual weaknesses, then you become a more seasoned team. If you just remove a problem, you may be replacing it with something much worse. You are the leader; it's up to you to create a winning team. Know your team members' strengths and weaknesses; learn their personality traits, and you will enjoy your position more than you thought possible. It really is about the people.

Life Application Review

Section Six

There is no greater variety of leadership than that found in sports. Between the coaching and managing, this venue brings together a great diversity of talent to form a team that plays as one. As a workplace leader you will be both coach and manager. You will have to take new talent and impart to them your wisdom and experience. For those seasoned team members, you as the manager will be required to bring all their skills and talents together to achieve a common goal. Again, one of the attributes of a great leader is his/her ability to recognize and grow the talent. You must be able to function as a team so that you may win as a team. There is a time to be a coach and a time to be the manager. You must learn the difference if you are to be a great leader.

Remember that the one in charge isn't necessarily the great leader. He/she may just be the boss. You must offer respect to the position no matter who is in charge. But if you are using that person as a role model for great leadership, then you will never be one. A leader will empower others, but a boss will seek power for self. Don't be a blame assessor. Empower people—leading them into their talents and abilities—by allowing them to follow you.

One of the greatest tragedies in life is the failure to reach one's full potential. There are so many gifted and talented people who never get to the place they were designed for. You can have all of the talent in the world, but if you cannot deliver when your talent is needed, then you are just another person with great potential. As great leaders we must desire to be the go-to person. We must always be assessing our circumstances so that we can make the necessary adjustments. According to some professional coaches, talent isn't all they're looking for. Know when to step it up and make it happen. Be the play maker.

The greatest skill you will have to master is your skill for understanding human behavior. You will have to be a student of people. Everything you do as a leader will be affected by or directly influenced by people. If you are a great student of people, you will be a great leader. We as individuals are affected by our encounters with what life has dealt to us. We perceive things differently. We apply various levels of importance to particular things. Nothing escapes the influence of conditioned behavior. So then you have to know your people in order to lead them to reach their full potential.

Section Seven

Yeah, I Hear You, But . . .

I will never forget the meeting during which this phrase came about. There were several of us team members sitting at a table going over some project strategies with the leader. All of us except the leader were volunteers agreeing to spend time to make this particular project work. It seemed that the more we tried to deal with some of the important issues, the more we kept losing ground. I guess you could say we ended up going around in circles. It was then that one of my colleagues made an amazing statement. He said to the leader, "I get it now! You keep saying, 'I hear you,' but you keep going back to what you want to do." This was when everything changed! We suddenly realized why we weren't getting anywhere. The leader was trying everything within his power to get what he wanted done by having us think what he wanted was our idea as well. Now, hear me out. It was a worthy project and definitely doable, but the way it was being done was shifting the focus from the real purpose of the project. All of the things that the leader wanted to do could be done, but priorities had to be established for the process to continue.

Let me explain it in a very simple manner. Let's suppose that I am the leader and I have assembled you along with the team together to cover some of the strategies for the project. We get into the meat of the operation. After much discussion and debate, we have discovered that in order to complete the project, we need *a piece of paper*. We have mapped out the size and type of paper, and we're now ready to proceed. You and the team, however, talk for a few moments and then say to me, the leader, "We would like for the *piece of paper* to be green." Now, remember, the color of the paper is irrelevant. We need the paper! I think for a moment and then say, "Green is good, but I think that red would be a much more suitable color for what we're doing." Do you see a problem with what I just did? As a leader I hope that you did. I just told my team that I didn't value them and that I didn't care what they thought. The color of the paper was irrelevant. Had it mattered, then more discussion would have been warranted. But in this case it didn't matter. You see, I hear you, but it is about what I want and not what the team needs.

How would I have solved the issue if the color of paper mattered? I would have included it in the priority of things to cover and would have come up with a series of colors that would have been acceptable and then let the team choose the color. The team still wins. But if the color doesn't matter, what does it profit me to take away a win for the team? Was it worth it, just so I could have it my way?

Be a leader who empowers your team to win and then celebrate the win with them. Listen to what they are saying and help direct those ideas to fit into the success of the project. By doing this you will find a team that is eager to win for you! And you will succeed in being a great leader.

Slow Is Smooth

You cannot attend very many leadership seminars without hearing the phrase "slow is smooth and smooth is fast." There is a powerful truth to this concept. The military uses it as a code of combat. In order to create a system of operations, you must create a series of actions that are done without hesitation. So how do you create those actions? I believe it is done by slow repetition. If you practice something slowly to get the technique down correctly, then the operation runs smoothly without mistakes, and it becomes instinctive. We all know that mistakes slow us down. If the action becomes performable without thought, then speed is a natural progression to the action. You basically react to the time lapse of the event. If you have to take time to figure out what to do in a split second of time, then mistakes are made and chaos usually ensues.

So how does what we've just talked about apply to great leadership? It's simple. A leader is a teacher, a trainer, and a guardian of knowledge. We have all heard the adage that if something is worth doing, it's worth doing right! That adage applies to every facet of leadership. You must always have a well-thought-out goal. There must be blueprints and strategies in place. Time lines are designed and organized to meet expectations along with goal projections. People are placed at strategic points as the leader methodically monitors the entire operation. If a leader goes into a project like a wild person, tossing bits of information around and putting people in places they don't belong, then the project is going to have to be done over or it will take much longer and cost more than if it had been done smoothly as well as methodically.

If you know what needs to be done then be the architect first. Make sure that everyone sees the overall plan and that everyone understands the process. Assign the right people according to their respective strengths, provide all of the right tools, and then implement the strategy: *slow is smooth and smooth is fast.* Time lines and interruptions will be met with automatic responses in the form of solutions and proper adjustments. Casualties will be kept to a minimum and cost will be kept within budget.

Remember that if your team fails, it means you failed! A leader can never walk into a situation, point a finger at a team member, and say it didn't work because of him/her. Do you know why? Because the leader planned the strategy, explained the mission, trained the team members, and then positioned them, approving them worthy for the task. This is why slow is smooth and smooth is fast. Be the leader who will take every task as a valuable one and then assemble the right team to take you to the next level. Your team is worth it; you are worth it!

Lowering Your Standards to Up Your Average

If you're looking for a way out of your situation, then you've just found it. If you're serious about excellence and a long career as a leader, then ignore this statement. Lowering your standards in order to increase your overall success is a cop-out. You see, when it's only about the numbers, then you're in survival mode. Survival mode simply means you have to do whatever it takes at that moment to survive that moment. It's no good! That moment will come and go no matter what you do. There is a solution for your current dilemma; you just haven't found it yet. So it is at these times that a leader must step back and start searching. And don't forget that there are those around you who are available to talk to and who will help you make the right decisions about your situation. You are never alone unless you want to be.

Your standard of excellence is what will separate you from others. The greatest enemy of excellence is compromise: whatever it takes to get by at the time. Consistency is the foundation for excellence. If you are consistent in the application of excellence in all things, then this will become instinctive. Creating a culture of excellence is a huge win for any leader. Since we have learned that culture is difficult to learn, then it must be a part of who we are at all times.

How does excellence translate to those under your influence? Let's look at this for a moment. First, if your instinct for excellence rings through in everything you do, then you automatically pull everyone else working with you to that level. They will look at everything they do with that same level of excellence in mind. Second, your own instinct for excellence will empower them to make decisions on projects that will eliminate wasted time. And third, commitment to excellence will attract a loyal base of trust that will work for you for years to come.

Today, more than in times past, we are seeing many leaders as well as their companies shifting into survival mode. Public officials compromise their character to stay one step ahead of the next opponent. They do whatever it takes, right or wrong, moral or immoral, to get it done. Most are doing what they feel is necessary for survival at any cost. Competition has been elevated to levels not seen in decades and now your word really does matter. How desperate are you and how low are you willing to drop your standards to win? When you're lowering your standards, there is one thing you can be certain of. You're not empowering anyone to do anything. Lowering your standards is a cheap fix and a sellout to your future. You are better than that!

Slow Motion Is Better Than No Motion

I believe that there is always a window of opportunity that makes itself available for the execution of every plan. You've probably heard of those who happened to be at the right place at the right time. But what you don't know is the number of times they have made that effort to be at that place at that particular time. Motion is the most critical factor in the execution of any plan.

Momentum must build as the plan is being worked. Yet for most, there is a stalling process that greatly hinders the progress of the plan. The key to success is motion, even if it is slow motion. You have to be moving toward the project in some form. I believe that one of the greatest tragedies is seeing people who have settled for something because it was the easy thing to do. Yet what most of us don't realize is that we spend the rest of our lives thinking about what we could have done. This is certainly more taxing than the original attempt at that one big thing! Imagine how many people have gone to their graves with talents and abilities that might have changed the world. But because there was no motion, there was no change.

Sometimes the most difficult task is the moving period. While I was working as a firefighter, I had the pressing task of rappelling off of tall condos in Cocoa Beach, Florida. The most difficult part was standing on the edge of the roof and leaning straight back to position myself to rappel down. Once I was over the edge, it was cake going down. But to stand on the edge of the condo and then lean back was really tough. All progress starts with motion, even if it takes a while to get up enough nerve to step out. It begins with getting to the rooftop, putting on the equipment, attaching the rope, moving toward the edge, and so on. Motion was the deciding factor, not the fear or pressure, just simple motion.

I believe one of the greatest examples of slow motion is the crawler-transporter that moved the Space Shuttles. This machine weighs 5,400,000 pounds. It has sixteen traction motors powered by four 1,341-horsepower (1,000 kW) generators in turn driven by two 2,750-horsepower (2,050 kW) Alco diesel engines. All of that amazing power moves the crawler at the unbelievable speed of less than 1 mile per hour. It takes the crawler five hours to go three and a half miles. Amazing, isn't it, to think that one of the slowest moving vehicles is used to carry the fastest?

You have to get this! The fastest that you may be able to go right now is in slow motion, but remember that it may be for just one leg of the journey. As long as something is moving toward the goal, then you're on your way. So get things together and mark your progress no matter how slow it may be. As long as you keep it moving, you will get there.

Life Application Review

Section Seven

Have you ever been in a position where your leader asks for your opinion but does exactly what he or she wants to do anyway? Frustrating, isn't it? Then don't be one of those leaders. There is nothing more lethal to creativity then to have the leader ask their team to brainstorm over a series of projects and then do what they had intended to do all along. You can work your own plan as a leader, but you cannot exclude your team when it comes to every detail. If you've hired a team that you don't have confidence in, then it doesn't speak very highly of you as a leader. It sounds like you have more of a control problem. I used to hear this phrase all of the time: "None of us are as smart as all of us." It is absolutely true. Be inclusive and manage your team with confidence in their talent and in your leadership skills.

If we can grasp the revelation of the phrase *slow is smooth*, then we have gained tremendous knowledge. Whether you think so or not, this statement is true. Some of the greatest expenditures in companies are the result of mistakes or miscalculations. We are in a hurry to meet a deadline and will do whatever we have to just to get it done. What we don't realize is that we are setting into motion more problems to deal with down the road. Nothing truly begins in chaos. Chaos is born out of a series of events or circumstances that have not been managed properly and have become uncontrollable. If we start a plan off smoothly, then we can build momentum while we build excellence at the same time. The basics are essential. You need to have a great plan, the right people doing what they do best, and steady smooth motion until the project is completed.

There is no way you can speak of standards without including character. Without character there is no way to measure standards. Character is the foundation upon which high standards are built.

This is what keeps you doing the right thing and protects truth. When there is the presence of great character, then there will be no compromise, no sellout or deceit. Instead, you will have only that which reflects the proper anatomy of great leadership. Never lower your standards to impress anyone. Stay the course, and you will never regret it because in time it will carry you through.

I am a firm believer in having all your ducks in a row before you start. But hey man, those ducks can keep you swimming in circles forever. You have to take some kind of step to get started. Put a plan together, get feedback on the plan, and then make adjustments to the plan. Add colorful pictures to the plan but get something going. You will discover that you actually create more anxiety from imagining all of the pitfalls than you do from the actual project.

Come on, now. You know what to do. Make sure you cover the basics. Have a great plan. Get a hold of the necessary tools. Put the right people in place and work the plan. There will be setbacks and hurdles to jump, but you're a leader and know how to deal with stuff. Even if you're at a crawler's pace to start with, you are still working the plan and that is forward motion. Before long, you will find yourself moving at Shuttle speed.

Section Eight

The Voice of Reason

REASON: An underlying fact or cause that provides logical sense for a premise or occurrence.

Ah, the voice of reason. That faithful friend who shows up just in the nick of time to give clear and precise direction, right? Wrong! If thought is open for interpretation, then how can reason be the savior of every situation? It can't. The voice of reason is your conscience. Your conscience is the sum-total of your thoughts expressed in the form of behavior. So then, where does the voice of reason come into play? The answer is: before the project is ever put on paper. The leader who thinks before he plans will not be left to chance, or worse. Leaders have, in today's information age, the ability to learn so much in a very short time, in some cases within minutes. Many take this knowledge and position themselves for the kill. They throw a plan together and blast into it like a raging bull. They are trying to make something happen fast so that they will succeed. What then?

If you have ever had the opportunity to sit down with successful leaders, you will find that they all have formulas of some kind, indicators that keep them focused on the goal. They will pass everything they do through these formulas and will never compromise on them, not even for one second. I remember attending a meeting with several millionaires. One of them was working on a charitable project. As he discussed this venture, one of the millionaires pulled out a billfold from the inside of his coat and laid thousands of dollars on the table and slid it over to the philanthropist. My friend just slid it back and said, "I will let you know when I need it." He later asked me what I thought about the incident and my response was bewilderment as to why he did not take it. He then told me that when someone offers you money, you shouldn't be quick to grab it because it might be the only money you will get from that person. He explained to me that if he appeared to be comfortable and not anxious around large amounts of money, then it made the person giving it comfortable as well. To them, this was just one small formula they used to test the waters. And remember everyone likes to get money back they had offered to give. The intent to them is just as rewarding.

The voice of reason is your where with all to be comfortable with your ability to lead. It means you are sure about the decisions you make, that your calculations have been thoroughly worked and that people trust you to make the call. You have to ask yourself if you are true to your formulas even when you are being tempted by emotional influences. This is what makes a leader great, the voice of reason that has been active from the beginning, ensuring that nothing was left to chance and that compromise was not an option. Now, don't get me wrong. There have been some pretty big deals that have happened that didn't make sense, but there was a plan and the risk was measured. No matter what you do, your conscience should be solid, immovable against outside influences and should provide a formula that equates success in the truest sense. Don't make plans for projects that have not been first established on foundations of reason, tested and proven to be the best they can be. We're counting on you!

The Art of Teaching Experience

Let me start by clarifying something here of great importance. Contrary to popular belief, it is almost impossible to teach experience! You may be able to explain the process well, but that is it. I have spent the last thirty years of my life working with young people. There is one constant that remains sure and that is: they all have to find out for themselves. I wish with everything in me that this were not the case, but it is and nothing will ever change it. If you have had the privilege of raising children, then you are an expert on this subject. First, you try to protect children by establishing boundaries. Then, you go through the descriptive reenactments of the dangers. These are nothing more than safer barriers that provide a cushioning for the impact of life. There is, of course, the constant interjection of the word *no* that will protect them from falls, burns, cuts, or worse. Yet in spite of all of these great insights and precautions, children do the exact opposite of what you tell them to do! What is it that made them not believe you or made them think they knew more? Their brains are still in the developmental stage. Common sense has not engaged their ability to reason things out. For the most part, they're still being governed by emotion. We must admit that it is human nature to want to know firsthand what the deal is. The serious side to this is that sometimes the cost for this personal knowledge is great and for some, even tragic.

So, what do you do to deal with this human tendency? The answer is that you train them to get through it and to reacquire the course. Remember that as leaders we are ever learning and applying experience to every situation and making the necessary adjustments to reach our goals. As I look back over the years, I remember young people who have gone on to capture their dreams. Whether it is teaching or flying, practicing law or finance, music or hundreds of other careers, the key truth that made the difference was each individual's passionate pursuit of his/her dream. Never give up! Even though those young people may have added more obstacles by not listening to the voice of experience, they made adjustments and moved on. They did not use obstacles as excuses for quitting on themselves and their dreams.

I remember when I first got my driver's license, I was sixteen years old. I was fortunate because my father had bought a '68 Camaro, and it was still in mint condition. My brother and I drove it to school every day. The big thing back then was noise. If it was loud, then it must be fast. So naturally I wanted that car to be loud. I remember discussing this truth with my dad and his response to me was that the noise was only going to get me a ticket. "Hey, what does he know, man? Times have changed!" Well, instead of listening to the wisdom of experience, I put loud pipes on that machine. The weekend finally came, and my friends and I wanted to take a short road trip. So off we went in that very loud '68 Camaro. I turned onto the interstate ramp and punched it. The noise was unbelievable. How cool was this? A short time later, I looked in my mirror and there before my eyes were flashing blue lights. You've got it! The Florida Highway Patrol bagged me. I pulled over and rolled down my window as the trooper approached. He explained to me how he was sitting there under the overpass and then heard this noise that reminded him of the weekend drag races. He didn't see me at first, but he heard me. That noise led him right to me. Well, I received a hefty fine and went right home to take the pipes off the car. The worst part wasn't the ticket; it was looking my father in the face and asking him for the money to help pay for it. He could have said, "I told you so," but he just shook his head. It is frustrating to watch others go through what could have been prevented if only the voice of experience was trusted.

In light of this simple truth, what will you do with knowledge that is being given to you? Like the rest of us, you will probably have to find out for yourself. A friend of mine used the illustration of a guy who walks around the corner and gets hit on the head with a bat. As he's rubbing his head, his friend Joe asks what happened. When he tells Joe, Joe responds by saying, "No way!" What does Joe do next? You've got it. He sticks his head around the corner to see and the same thing happens to him. Before long, you have a whole line of people rubbing their heads. You just have to find out for yourself. But remember that when you do, you've got to get back up, dust yourself off, put some ice on your head, and press on because you are a leader and you have a dream to catch.

Surviving Is Not Growing

Simply surviving is the prelude to death. It is nothing more than the hemorrhaging of life. It is the destroyer of dreams. In order to live you have to move beyond surviving. You may think this is a bit strong, but believe me; it is the truth. You must get this here and now! If you are just surviving, then you are losing ground in life. Remember. This may be where you are right now, and you may be making the necessary adjustments to get by, but your mind must be focused on your future. You are not just surviving, you are processing your options, you are taking inventory of your resources, and you are working out a plan that will take you to the next level. A leader will never just survive.

Surviving will cause you to settle. Settling is compromise, and compromise is having only half the dream. Everything worthwhile will cost you something. There is nothing wrong with getting rocked and having to get your senses back. You may be saying that you've had a major setback. Okay, then step back and assess your situation. Recognize that you have been through a difficult and possibly life-altering event. But at some point you must find your way through it and move forward. Listen. It doesn't mean that you take the setback lightly or even that you have to forget it, but you must press forward. Just as an athlete has to exercise after an injury despite great pain, likewise we have to exercise our minds to refocus and move ahead after a setback.

Remember the discussion about the GPS in the chapter about recalculating? The most difficult task at hand is trying to find out where you are. You know where you have come from and where you want to go. The place in which you may presently exist is very painful. In fact, it may be so painful that you don't know where you are in relation to the other two points. This is when you have to trust in your indicators.

I remember some time ago talking with my son about flying. He was sharing with me how difficult it was to trust in the instrument over what you think you can see. One of his flying jobs required him to fly out over the Gulf to the various oil rigs. Often, the weather would change without warning, and he couldn't see a thing. He said that visibility was calculated by yards instead of miles. It was then he had to fly with the instruments. At times, everything in him wanted to do just the opposite of what his instruments were telling him to do. But he said that the instruments were absent of one particular thing that we have: emotions and feelings that somehow make us want to do certain things without sufficient facts. The mind may be convinced that it can make the right decision, but without all of the facts and information, feeling is not enough. And at times it can be lethal.

There are indicators and instruments all around you. Information and support are readily available to you through friends and others who have endured similar setbacks. If you choose to simply survive because you cannot muster enough strength to do anything else, then let someone help you up. They will have enough strength for both of you until you are able to move forward. Please, do not just survive. Your gifting and talent was given to make the world a better place. And don't forget to look behind you. People are still following you because they believe in you.

Preparing the Square Peg
for the Round Hole

Don't worry, we all have to make constant adjustments to accommodate change. The fact that we work with people means that we have to constantly readjust. I believe in the business world it is known as "**flexibility**." Yeah, I'm sure of it. So, as a leader the question now is, how flexible are you supposed to be? The answer is simple. You must be flexible enough to put a square peg into a round hole and make it look like it belongs there. After all, you are a leader and are looked upon to do the impossible. Contrary to popular belief, leaders are called upon daily to make decisions that would make the average person faint of heart. But for the true leader, he/she thrives on making it work. The real art is making the square peg look like it belongs in the round hole in the first place.

You will seldom enjoy the opportunity of having everything go the way you had prepared for it to go so many weeks or months prior. You spend time making sure everyone gets it. You make sure everyone has the tools, you map out the execution, and then everything changes. Yet you have to come up with the same results as if you had planned the whole thing out with this scenario in mind. This is why you always mentally prepare for change. It is not something that is productive or even healthy, but you must anticipate the possibility.

Coaches also have to prepare their players for what they call, "**sudden change**." Imagine, you have just held your opponent at the goal line for four downs. It seems as though the momentum has shifted to your side. But the very next play your quarterback throws an interception and they get the ball right back. If you have not prepared the team for this, they will give up right then and there.

But if you have been running drills on sudden change, then they will automatically go into their training mode and will focus on defense and not on losing. Think about the meetings, dinners and events that have been planned to the minute and then boom, the call comes in to make the changes in a fraction of the time it normally takes. Oh, and by the way, it needs to be just as good as if it were planned from the beginning. Preparation and conditioning makes all the difference in coming apart or taking it to the next level.

I'm not particularly fond of backup plans either because making one means you have to shift your focus to something that may never happen. So I am more in favor of someone who takes into consideration the creative aspect of human error and human nature. This means having the kind of mind-set that would leave room to step back, reassess the situation, and immediately move toward a solution. Remember that a round peg starts out as a square one anyway. You see? You're already getting it! All you have to do is shave the corners, and it'll fit like a glove.

Don't forget you are leading people. They do matter, and it is important to bring them to the place where they too can problem solve. Your people are a reflection of your leadership. You may find that some of them have become masters at fitting difficult things together. Show them you appreciate them. As you empower them, you empower your future as a leader. Remember that your greatest asset is your team.

Life Application Review

Section Eight

There truly is no greater watchdog than your own conscience, that is, if you have one. It will always call for you to do the right thing. Imagine a world where people did the right thing because it was the right thing to do. No special recognition, no rewards or promotions, only the gratification of being honest and doing the right thing. Character would certainly flourish. It is not that way, however, so you must bring your conscience with you. That voice of reason must guide you through your life in all that you do. It is the captain of your decision making.

As a leader you must create some type of a checks-and-balances system that protects you. Your decision-making process must pass through a series of thought as well as discussion. It is far easier to begin than it is to stop, tear down, go back, and rebuild. Remember that others are following you, and what you do impacts them as well. Don't just do things because you can; make things count in a big way.

Be teachable as you teach others. If we could somehow get others to believe what we are saying, it would save all of us a lot of needless frustration. Unfortunately, most people have to find out for themselves. Find creative ways to teach. You live in a world where information is a mouse click away. There is nothing you can't learn about within just a few minutes.

I remember something my business and law instructor shared with the class one day, and I will probably never forget it. He made a simple statement that was weighted with truth. He said, "Ignorance of the law is no excuse." It doesn't matter how little you know about the law in different states or even countries. Whether you're spending time there or just passing through, you need to know what you can and cannot do.

Even in a tough economy it seems that we become satisfied with just getting through the day. Companies are closing down all around you, and you struggle with the possibility that yours is next. It is in these times that you must become more creative than ever before. If you are just surviving, then you are no longer growing. As a leader, you by your very nature are looking ahead to the future. Let's not forget those who faced a time of difficulty and yet rose above it. Henry Ford was in a difficult situation due to a tough economy, high employee turnover, and absenteeism. He did something that turned the industrial world upside down. He doubled his employee's wages and cut the price of the Model T. Overnight, people began scrambling to get hired. Guess what the end result was? First, Ford's employee turnover and absenteeism rates were drastically cut. Second, his employees became his new customers. And third, the quality of workmanship went through the roof. Why? Because his employees were building the cars they were buying. It was creativity at its best.

Nothing is ever what it seems to be. You can plan and cover every base and still something will be off. What is the solution to this dilemma? The solution is called preparedness. As a leader you will constantly be making adjustments for reaching your goals. Remember what you are in pursuit of and that there are many ways to get there. When interruptions come or things aren't what you expected, step back, regroup, and then get focused on the goal. And don't forget the ice.

Section Nine

The Stabilizing Factor

It is no great revelation that balance is the key to all things. Even though the need for balance is widely understood, it is seldom practiced. We all need balance. Everything you do is first processed through your mind. What we put our hands to is merely the expression of thought that brings us to the important topic of the mind. Your mind is the tool of your trade, and so you are constantly feeding it with knowledge. You process information at warp speeds, and you seldom disengage your mind from service. Is this a bad thing? It is if you cannot tell me the name of your wife and the ages of your kids. If you have neither, then I want to know how the bike ride was last weekend or how the water was at the beach and so on.

You must know that creativity comes from some of the most bizarre situations. I never really understood how significant balance was until I watched an archer shoot his bow in competition. As he steadied his bow, the stabilizers attached to each side allowed him to focus directly onto the target. There was no movement, no variation from his sights. As he methodically released his grip on the string, the arrow flew and found its mark. You see, the stabilizers assist in sudden eruptions of wind or movement. Without the stabilizers to counterbalance the interruptions, there is uncontrolled motion that will certainly affect the outcome of your aim.

We all know there's not enough time in a day to do all we need to do, but we also know that we can't judge production by movement. If we are not at one hundred percent, then we can assume it will take us longer to get to where we need to be. On the other hand if we have been refreshed, then we can move farther in a shorter amount of time, and as a result we have increased our productivity. I believe one of the truest phrases I've ever heard is this one: "Being busy doesn't mean you're productive." As a leader you may see a busy office, but how do you know it's producing? What tools do you use to measure productivity? I'm not talking about micromanaging in any way. What I'm doing here is holding up a mirror. You can find ways to be busy 24/7 and even feel good about it. But really, what are you feeling good about? If you're keeping people at work and you have to pay overtime, then you are not a good manager of time, budgets, or people. There may be times when you have to make an exception due to increased demands for product or scheduling setbacks, but overtime should never be something an employee counts on as regular pay. Remember that if you keep employees there, they deserve the pay. If they're there because of poor time management, you need some balance.

There will be unexpected interruptions no matter how well you plan, so what is your stabilizing factor? Find it and make sure you look after it. It needs as much attention as your work. Life, you will find, is a gift. There is no guarantee as to how long you will have it the way it is, so enjoy it. Step back and asses how things are and then set that thing aside and have a little balance with all that stress. Life is good!

How's My Driving?

We have all seen them. They're on just about every commercial vehicle you see on the road. They are the "How's My Driving?" bumper stickers. But let's face it; the only time you would ever call the number is if that commercial vehicle cut you off or angered you in any way. We never call to say how great a job the driver is doing. It is not how we are programmed. If those drivers invade our space, someone is going to know about it. But we seldom take the effort to celebrate when someone else is doing well.

As a creative leader you will not survive without feedback. You need to hear how well you are doing. Listen to me here because this is so very important to your success. The creative aspect of your brain needs the support. You are probably your worst critic anyway and may at times doubt your abilities. This means you are already anticipating negativity. You see an expression on a team member's face, and you automatically think it is because of your leadership. It is probably because they have a teenager at home. But you are convinced his or her facial expression has something to do with you.

Please do not become self-destructive. It is a common tendency for creative people to become so self-critical that they begin to sabotage their own futures. This is why it is important to surround yourself with those who believe in you and see your leadership as positive. Remember that as a leader you are a student of people or, more importantly, human behavior.

Like so many others, I have learned that there are many different types of people out there. I will attempt to put my own names and descriptions on different types of behavioral issues that may help you remember them. These people do, whether you choose to believe it or not, affect you in a big way. The first group we will call the "**whywouldyouans**." These are the individuals who are happy with the way things are. They are comfortable with where they're at and have no desire to move ahead nor would they encourage anyone else to do so either. You will get no support from them. The second group of people we will call the "**it'stoohardians**." These people are excuse experts. They are top in their field and are ready to give you many reasons why you will not see your dreams come true. They are also experts in the art of ambush. They seem to always know when you are the most vulnerable. And the third group to beware of is the most dangerous. These are usually the ones who influence us the most. They are called the "**youcan'tdoitans**." Stay clear of these subtle but dangerous individuals because they are dream killers. They will take from you every positive thought, every creative idea, and ultimately rob you of confidence in your own abilities. These individuals must never have the final say when it comes to chasing your dreams.

At the end of the day, the only one responsible for you, is you! Your decisions will always be the ones that take you where you want to go. If what you're in pursuit of is honorable and empowering to others, then you have to find those who will support you in doing it, those you can call when you doubt yourself. Look for someone who walks in with a smile, and when he or she says, "I believe in you," you know they really mean it. Remember that you are the leader and there are many who are anxious to follow. Stay the course and go chase your dream; it's waiting for you.

The Best Excuse, Ever!

Get your notes out because you really need to remember this one. The best excuse you will ever have for failure is **you**! That's right! It's just that simple. You can't find a better source for excuses than you. After all, there is no one who knows you better than you and who knows more about what you've been through. And there is no one who knows what your breaking point is, better than you. Yeah, there is no better excuse for your future than you.

Well, how did I do? Did I get the point across? Then let's just leave it at that, enough said: finished, finite, over and done with. Let's move on.

Hocus Focus
(Don't Just Chase the Dream—Live the Journey)

Remember to stay focused. If you keep your eye on the prize, then you won't run the risk of getting distracted. Learn to run your race and not someone else's. Without fail there are countless athletes who spend so much time watching their competition that they lose sight of their goal. I remember our track coach telling us that we had to slow down in order to look back at our competitors, which meant we were letting them catch up. It's human nature, yes, but it is also the thief of victory. You must believe that you are better than the competition anyway, so your only focus should be on your level of performance and getting that prize, whatever it is. Loss of focus means loss of concentration, which means you are not at a hundred and ten percent. If you're not at a hundred and ten percent, then you are average like everyone else.

If you stop to think about it, we use the performance of others to measure our own. Why cheat yourself out of your best? There is nothing more motivating than to see athletes breaking their own world records. They're no longer in competition with others; they now compete against themselves. That, dear leader, is awesome!

Winning is contagious. There is something within the human makeup that gives individuals the need to celebrate. Humans by nature want somebody to win at something, anything. Celebration is a form of participation which in turn fills the void we have to feel success. Why not be the one that everybody is celebrating over? Better yet, why not be the person who brings others with them? If you win, then your team wins. If you win, then there is someone out there who wants to be like you. You then inspire others to go beyond their limitations and leave the competition behind.

At the end of the day, we all have that place we go where we just sit and try to make sense of what we just lived through. Most of this time is spent on the problems and failures we had. We focus on what didn't get done. Some of us even spend the time gathering information on the competition and come to the conclusion that we didn't do that bad. And once again we find solace in the measuring of our progress by the lack of others. If we continue this pattern, then we will never truly find fulfillment. We will end up chasing an endless dream. Don't just chase the dream; live the journey. If you cannot appreciate what it took to fulfill the dream, then the dream will never be what you thought it would be. You will never be satisfied. All of the hard work, the sacrifices, all of the people who inspired and helped you, they are all a part of the dream. All of it is what adds the value to your dream.

There will always be obstacles that are beyond your control, but your mind should not be one of them. Don't forget that if what you are in pursuit of is noble and worthy of recognition, then it warrants doing your best. Take a look around you and really appreciate those who have inspired or helped you. Look at where you have come from to be where you are today. And when you hold that prize in your hand, you will be able to celebrate the journey that made it so much more valuable. Stay focused on the prize and not on those you are competing with. You be the one to set your own standard and always take time to savor each moment, because all of it makes up the dream. Remember to live the journey.

Life Application Review

Section Nine

Balance is something we all need. I personally believe that balance will help increase creativity. Sometimes if you step away from something, you get a whole new perspective of it. Each individual must determine what that balance is and how much time he/she will dedicate to it. In essence the balance becomes the stabilizing factor in life. Remember that everything holds value based on its relevance. For instance, if you are on your deathbed, suddenly what you pursued most of your life holds little value. Instead, you wish you had spent more time with loved ones. Others often wish they had fished more or taken more time to spend with friends. Everything is relative to the moment. As our situations change so also does our perspective. So all of us, no matter what dream or passion we are chasing, must find something that becomes the stabilizing factor in our lives be it a loved one, family, friends, or even a hobby. We must have it. What is your stabilizing factor?

Isn't it amazing how all of us have the need for approval? No one deals well with rejection, and I mean no one. We are creatures of community; it's how we're made. We all have a need to fit in. I think that a large part of the need for approval is programmed into us at an early age. As children we were celebrated for our first smiles. Our first steps were broadcast as if we had walked on the moon. And our first spoken words melted the hearts of our parents. As time went on every little new thing we mimicked became something to be celebrated. We learned later in life that no one celebrates human behavior anymore. It becomes what is expected of you; grow up we're told! Yet we all still need to know we are doing well.

It is important to the leader to get feedback. Without feedback the leader will not know how well they're doing. Leaders need to know the attitude of the team and their position of loyalty. This does not mean you surround yourself with "yes" people either. As a leader you must be secure enough in your position to take constructive criticism. Remember that you built the team and you need to hear them out. If you did your job well, they will add to the plan and not take away.

When the day is done, never let the reason for not obtaining your dream be you. There are a lot of things you have no control over, but *you* shouldn't be one of them. Don't beat yourself; you have to live with you the rest of your life!

Without focus you cannot stay the course. The journey is difficult enough without distractions, let alone focusing on those around you. If you measure your progress against the failures of those around you, then you are average. You must measure your progress by your own goals. No one will ever hold you to a higher standard than you will. Having said that, make sure that you understand that the journey is part of the prize. You can pursue a dream your entire life, but if you fail to see what got you there, then the dream is never enough. Always take a moment to step back and see the bigger picture. In it you will find the many faces of those who somehow influenced your journey and who made your dream possible. You may find, after all, that they are the ones you are really leading.

Section Ten

Key Pitfalls of Leaders

Approval
(The Need for It)

For whatever reason, all leaders seek approval, and without it they feel utterly lost. To say that the need for approval is not a vital part of their makeup would be an understatement. But one must also realize that there is a healthy need for approval and an unhealthy need. The unhealthy need becomes an obsession that leads to self-destruction. We discussed in this book how important the influences around us were. These influences have shaped who we've become, be it good or bad. Now I cannot say that we have the right to blame those influences for our failures, but they have definitely played a part in our growth as leaders.

Approval is healthy for the leader. Leaders need feedback to know that they are being accepted. A more creative leader—or let's say, a visionary—really has to have reinforcement on a regular basis. Without it they may feel rejected. Insecurity is also a common trait of some leaders. They need to know that the team has their back at all times. Now, these are not necessarily bad things. They're just some of the characteristics that need constant monitoring.

Leaders are seldom afraid of failure. They have recognized the risk but feel that the accomplishment of the task at hand is worth the risk. Non-leaders will use the risk as justification for just sitting it out. True leaders can't be held down. They will find ways to make things happen; it's just what they do.

So how do you find the balance for needing approval? I think that the real balance to this whole thing is to separate one's search for personal approval from the need for professional approval. The personal search for approval for the most part is the result of not having it in your youth. You know what I'm talking about, don't you? For most of us, we chased after that "well done, I'm proud of you" affirmation from the proverbial parent or guardian. That alone for a period of time is what drove us to succeed and rise to the top. Later, the thrill of success in itself is what drove us.

For those who were never able to be satisfied in their personal searches for approval, know that it could create difficulties for you as the leader. The important thing you must know is how to differentiate between the need for personal approval and the need for professional approval in order to go where you need to go. If you do not, you will destroy what you have accomplished, and you will create a lot of collateral damage as well.

Healthy approval allows leaders to get their bearing on progress as well as to let them know that they are appreciated. A great lesson to be learned here is for great leaders to remember that those they are leading need approval as well. Approval is free, it doesn't cost anything, and it is one of the most productive things you can do. Giving approval is not a sign of weakness. It shows to those you lead that you are not insecure but rather confident not only in your abilities, but in those of the team as well. Look around you. You're not alone, and you are going to make it. By the way, great job!

Neglect

Neglect is simply the absence of true passion. The word *passion* comes from the Latin word *patior* meaning to suffer or endure. This is a fitting definition, when you think about it. If you are passionate about something, you will endure certain sufferings in order to posses it. So then, what causes you to neglect something you were once so passionate about? In essence it is the loss of personal touch. This is how you lose the passion. Let me say here that neglect is one of the most painful things to be the recipient of; it really hurts and it leaves permanent scars.

I am not going to touch on all of the areas of neglect that we might create as leaders, as you probably know what most of them are already. So you fill in the blanks as we go. Our common cry as leaders is that there is just not enough time in one day to get all of the things done that need to be done. Trust me, dear leader. There will never be enough time and never enough workers or tools to get it all done. So then, you must as the leader control what is the acceptable amount of progress. This is not a compromise. This is called *strategy*.

Remember what we've said over and over again: being busy doesn't necessarily equate with being productive. Keeping this in mind will help you do something else that is also very important, and that is prioritizing your time and workload. Being a great leader doesn't mean that you have to get a certain amount of things done in one day. Remember that leadership is not about a particular job; it is about a journey. It's a journey where you empower others to go with you. So this means that you plan projects, and place people in positions to perform tasks in certain order at particular times to meet a deadline. As you monitor progress, you can also call for adjustments as well as allow for changes. If you as a leader have assembled a great team who believe you are a great leader, then you will have great results.

Don't lose touch with the things that matter the most; you will regret it. Besides, you need the balance. Make the time to tend to those things that complete your life. There is one truth I have come to believe above many others and that is, you will always make time for what you are passionate about. It doesn't matter what's at stake, you will make the time. You see, it makes sense. We neglect things and people because we have lost the passion we once had by losing touch with them. I'm reminded of the huge ships that travel the oceans. As they set the compass, a small rudder keeps their course true, but if that rudder is off even one degree, things change. You may not notice it at first, but over the course of days you will end up miles off course. Someone has to have their hands on the controls. Maybe time has revealed to you that you are not on the path you started out on. Reset your course and place your hands back on the wheel of your life. Take a minute to step back and find your focus. You're already a great leader; you just need some personal touch. Reconnect with something you have lost the passion for. When you do, then use your head to keep things prioritized. You're not that far off course, at least not yet.

Abuse

There are many different kinds of abuse. The previous topic on neglect is a form of abuse. Leaders can be abusive and not be intentional in doing it. Some leaders just don't care, as long as they are winning. But I am sure that this is not you. So let's talk about ways to prevent the abuse of those you are leading. I'm going to categorize some different types of abuse we create as leaders that may make it easier to relate to. First, we might create abuse through lack of recognition. I have seen over the years many people who make companies successful are the least paid and never recognized. Look at companies who rely on customer service for example. Their greatest asset is the employee who is waiting on you. You can buy the product in any number of stores, but how you're treated during the purchase or transaction of the product can make or break your patronage. These people on the front lines are the ones making it happen for the team. I have always been amazed at how coaches will say over and over again that they win or lose as a team. It's about the team, the team, the team. And yet, at the end of the game, the coaches give the game ball to one person. It is usually the guy who is in the skill position, the guy who has his hands on the ball. This process never made sense to me. Is it really about the team? Don't neglect your team members because their positions are not visible. If they are a part of your team, then they need to know how much you appreciate what they do.

Another form of abuse is verbal abuse. You don't have to be a rocket scientist to figure this one out. You know when you are guilty of verbal abuse. It's wrong, and it should not happen! I have said this before, but it warrants repeating. Just because your position empowers you to do so, you still don't have the right to abuse others. I believe that rebuking an employee in front of other employees shows a weakness in your leadership abilities. It is a cheap attempt to show everyone that you have power. Doing so may even reveal that you are somewhat of a pretender. This would not be a good thing. Remember that as leaders, we are to empower others not destroy them.

Now, I don't mean there should be no discipline. If discipline is warranted, then pull the employee into the office with a supervisor, if necessary, and deal with the situation, but never discipline in front of the rest of the team. The team will lose respect for you and will not forget it.

I remember a leader who was so critical of everyone's input at staff meetings that the staff just quit participating, and the leader couldn't figure out why. The staff became gun-shy. Never throw a hand grenade when a sniper rifle is needed. The collateral damage is severe and there will be no one left to lead.

This next particular form of abuse is seldom discussed. Nevertheless, it is abusive. I call it the "dangling carrot" abuse. There are some leaders who dangle carrots in front of their team members to get them to perform. This is not a good way to get more productivity out of your team. I believe that the use of empty promises goes back to character issues. For the team this form of abuse is a morale killer and causes a great deal of backstabbing. If you are a leader and you want a bad nickname, then just keep making empty promises. It's not wrong to utilize true incentives, but make sure what you offer is possible to do. One of the greatest compliments you can be paid as a leader, is to have a new team member tell you that everyone says that you do what you say you will do. Now, that's the making of a great leader. Don't hold people out over the precipice of promises to just hang there. Don't use a dangling carrot to serve up false hope only to crush the spirit by not delivering. Wait until you can make something happen before you use it as an incentive. And remember that nicknames aren't necessarily a good thing.

Influence

You are a reflection of who you have been with. We are greatly affected by those who have significance in our lives. Even as leaders we are followers in that we aspire to be like someone we admire. Influences shape not only our attitudes but also our course in the pursuit of our dreams. There are good influences, bad influences, positive influences, and negative influences. All of them go into shaping who we become on our journey toward the prize. Chuck Swindoll said, "Life is 10% of what happens to us and 90% of how we deal with it." Whether you choose to accept it or not, you are greatly affected by those around you; right now, at this moment, they are affecting you.

Often, we tend to gravitate toward influences that are easiest to imitate. There is a danger inherent in following after the influences that cost little or nothing. And most certainly danger in those influences that tell you status quo is acceptable. If you are not aggressively moving ahead, then you are going back; there is no standing still.

I remember having a friend who usually saw the worst in everything. He was generally a miserable guy. I thought that by hanging out with him, I could be a more positive influence on him. Well, it turned out that I was right to some degree, but when I left, I usually took something with me. As soon as I got home, my mom would say that she could tell that I was hanging out with so and so. I would ask her how she knew, and she would say that I was not myself, and that she could see it on my face. It was true; it would take me some time to get back up and positive about the future. While I was helping him, he was draining me.

Negativity is your greatest enemy for reaching your goals. A dream can be crushed with a simple negative remark. What are you reading and is it helping to grow and empower your thought process.

The atmosphere you are in supplies the drive for your dream. It will become the determining factor as to whether or not you are where you're supposed to be when destiny seeks you out. There is a quote from the Bible that holds absolute truth, and I want to share it. *"Death and life are in the power of the tongue."* (Proverbs 18:21). We often fail to see that what we think matters to people. I think sometimes what an awesome responsibility it is to have others value what I say. So much so that it influences their decision making and those decisions ultimately affect the rest of their lives. How can we so casually speak without thinking?

I have found in life, maybe a little too late, that I have spent too much time around people who've said, "You can't," instead of those who would say, "Let's see how you can!" You see, it is easy to say you can't because it relieves you of all responsibility to help. You can brush your hands clean and move on; that is what most people do. But how powerful of an influence are those who say, "I believe you can, and I want to be the first to help." Those are the influences that have helped change our world. You may never know their names or may never see their faces, but they are there standing behind all those who are holding their dreams in their hands.

You may have experienced unhealthy influences in your life. Those influences have made your journey more difficult and most certainly more lonely. You see now, however, that you ultimately have the choice. Surround yourself with those who will encourage you even when you want to quit. Keep your mind focused on the prize, and show your team that your dream was more than just an empty thought. Show them that they were the part that made it worth the while. You must see that you're worth it; their worth it!

Alienation

Remember the old cliché, "It's lonely at the top"? Well, I don't believe it was meant to keep leaders from other team members. I believe it means that sometimes you as the leader are left with the final decision and all of the responsibility rests with you. There is definitely a big difference. A lot of leaders do alienate themselves from their team members. I have heard leaders say, "I can't be their friend because I'm their boss." No, you probably have a different circle of friends and have different interests.

Just because you are a leader, however, doesn't mean that you cannot develop a relationship with your team. Why not be in a position to ask your team member how his/her family is doing and call the employee and family members by name? How many times do we as leaders stand up and say we really care and say, "I love you guys." Yet when a team member is facing difficulties or has a loved one in the hospital, we never stop to ask how things are going. You must realize that whatever is going on at home is affecting what's going on at work. Make a phone call or stop by a team member's work area and ask how things are going or if they are in need of anything; it really is the leader thing to do. And by the way, if you are going to use the excuse of having too many employees, it's not going to work. All of us know that you have your levels of responsibilities, and then there are those under you who have others under them and so on. The point is that everyone should be looked after on every level.

I remember a situation in which an employee wanted to do something for his leader to show him how much he appreciated his job. Now I know that this is not to be encouraged, but it happened anyway. The employee had seen this book holder that was made of six different types of wood sitting on a friend's desk. He asked his friend where he purchased it and was told that he'd had it made. The employee asked if he thought the man would make another one for him. He said he would call the man and ask him. To make a long story short, the employee made sacrifices and saved the money to purchase the expensive book holder for his leader. This poor employee didn't know what was about to hit him. He picked up the gift and took it straight to his leader. When the leader saw it, he inquired as to its purpose. The employee told him it was to hold his books while he read. The response from the leader was less than encouraging. He simply said, "Interesting." The very next day the gift was under the stairwell with the things to be placed in storage. If you as a leader do not value positive response from employees that supersedes their paychecks then you've really missed it.

Don't think for one moment that your team can't tell when you're not listening or you don't care. For example, there is nothing more inconsiderate than to be looking off while a team member is talking to you. You may have other things on your mind, but if you didn't alert the employee to that fact, then you need to hear him/her out. After all, you do care, right? This is definitely a form of abuse. Think about this for a moment. What an awesome responsibility it is when your opinion adds worth to someone's ideas. Always listen to what a team member is saying. It is important not only to them but to you as the leader. Show appreciation for what they do for you. It matters and will go a long way when you have to call on that person to step it up.

No leader is an island. You have gifts and talents that go beyond your workplace that will enhance the quality of life for those around you. Go on, make some friends. We all need to belong.

A Final Thought

Well what do you think? The bottom line is you're the one who has the power to make the right decisions. Your choice is, well, your choice. Wisdom gained from experience coupled with good counsel should help you make the right choices. Those choices will lead you to the top, and you should be able to look behind and see that a crowd is with you.

Life is seldom free of difficulties as well as major setbacks. Being a leader does not mean you will never stumble. What it does mean is that the same qualities that have made you a great leader will also provide firm ground for you to find your footing again. One thing you have probably already learned is that life is unfair. No one's perfect, people will let you down just as you have let others down, and nothing is ever what it seems to be. So what? Those are not the reasons why you are leading. These are merely obstacles that you will turn into opportunities to grow through. The truth must always be your compass and perseverance must be your guide. Together, these strengths will see you past your difficulties and into your dreams.

This book started off by emphasizing the importance of building a foundation of character. And so it is fitting that we go back to character to seal the deal. Who are you? Where are you from? What happened to you, and how did you deal with it? If there were no obstacles or boundaries keeping you from your dreams, what would you be doing? All of these questions make up who you are. Remember, when you step up into a leadership position, you are introducing everyone to their new leader. That leader, being you, who's been forged and molded into the person you are today. All of life's encounters—good or bad, right or wrong—have had an influence on you. You have been affected by all of them. The difficult thing is to see how good of a leader they have made you.

You have gifts and talents that have been seasoned by the influences around you. You have heard over and over again that a true leader is someone who empowers others. This, as you already know, is a choice. There are always opportunities to be exclusive and to make the focus only about you on your journey to bigger things. But remember that if you plan on being around for a while, the people you take with you can make all of the difference in the world. Because you empowered them to reach their full potential, they are now at places in their fields to have the power to position you. Those you've empowered are only an email, text message or phone call away from making the difference in a win or lose situation. Nothing ever just happens; it just doesn't. There will always be a sequence of events that have led up to the happening; you just never know what all of them are.

As we've discussed before, destiny has everything to do with positioning. Destiny may show up the day that you decide to stay home, and you would never know the difference. Just the thought of that makes me feel weak at the knees. As long as you do everything in your power to be a great leader, then destiny will find you. I do not feel that success is selective by any means. I believe that passion attracts success and that if someone is passionate about something, it means they are there when destiny arrives. Remember, there is always going to be a time for quitting. It will never be too late to do that, but that's not true with winning. When it is all said and done, winning comes down to this: you are the designer, the architect, and the builder of your own future. Opportunities come along to set up the win. You must know that you have done everything to be there to capitalize on that opportunity: no excuses, no what ifs, and no I-didn't-knows. The possibilities are there, but the choice is yours; make the right one! Oh, and by the way, leadership really does look good on you.

About the Author

As an ordained minister, Dave Dungan has spent much of his time inspiring others. Whether he's creating ministries to equip inner-city kids to find their purpose, helping pastors to grow their churches or business owners to grow their businesses, Dave realizes you can do none of them without great leadership. Dave currently holds credentials with the IFCA (International Fellowship of Christian Assemblies). For the past thirty years, Dave and his wife Debbie have committed themselves to a variety of ministries. After spending more than thirteen years working with inner-city kids in the Boston area, they have shifted their focus toward helping pastors expand their ministries. With the church's growing need for leadership training and for the creation of small groups, this ministry move for Dave and Debbie was a perfect fit. Most recently, they have assisted pastors with the training of new leaders for the launching of additional campuses. All of this has paved the way for expanding into the entrepreneurial field where leadership training is a must. With the release of "*Don't Follow Me, I'm the Leader,*" Dave is now working on his third book scheduled to be released in the fall of 2012.

Dave is also the author of the newly released book, "***An Offering Made by Fire.***"